A SEQUEL OF THE WASLALA ROBBER STORIES

THE PRICE

Pablo Yoder

The Price
Copyright © 2012 Vision Publishers

ISBN-10: 1-932676-25-2
ISBN-13: 978-1-932676-25-9

Also available as E-book:
ePUB-10: 1-932676-57-0
ePUB-13: 978-1-932676-57-0

ePDF-10: 1-932676-58-9
ePDF-13: 978-1-932676-58-7

Printed in the United States of America

Cover Design: Lydia Zook
Text Layout and Design: Lanette Steiner

All scriptures taken from the King James Version.

For special discounts on bulk purchases, please contact:
Vision Publishers Orders by phone: 877.488.0901

For Information or Comments, Please Contact:
Vision Publishers
P.O. Box 190
Harrisonburg, VA 22803
Phone: 877.488.0901
Fax: 540.437.1969
E-mail: orders@vision-publishers.com
www.vision-publishers.com
(See order form in back)

Holmes Printing Solutions
8757 County Road 77 -- Fredericksburg, Ohio 44627
888.473.6870

TABLE OF CONTENTS

DEDICATION

I dedicate this book to my dear wife, who was willing to obey the toughest of God's commands: Love your enemies. Dearling, you loved the robbers who threatened to kidnap your husband several times, who held him at gunpoint, who threatened to harm your precious daughters, who stole so many of your belongings, and who even molested you once. Though you called it your personal Calvary, your love for Christ gave you compassion for the robbers every time they harassed you—not once, but over forty times!

I love you, Euni, for the brave woman God made you! To Him be all the honor and glory!

FOREWORD

The Price is the strangest book I have ever written. It verges on the bizarre, and as the old adage says, "Truth is often stranger than fiction."

Years ago, even during our special robber time between 1995 and 2000, this story was in the making. After that time, during our special rest in our little Garden of Eden in Waslala, the facts leaked out. God not only showed us who some of the robbers were who harassed us during that time, but He let us know what happened to some of them. For some reason, I was intrigued enough to follow the leads and dig out the facts. It was then that I felt God nudging me to write a sequel to the *Angels* series. Thus *The Price* was born.

I admit that the research for this book was also one of the strangest things I have ever done, but I thoroughly enjoyed it. Yes, it seemed strange to hunt people down and ask strange questions about their deceased relatives. I had to do it so that the stories would contain the true facts, and not just hearsay.

It was even a dangerous mission. Asking violent people probing questions is not the safest practice in Nicaragua. My family felt nervous when I left again and again, sometimes traveling into remote places. But through it all I clearly sensed

God's protection, and it gave me a unique opportunity to witness to people who need the Lord.

The day I spent in El Cuá with Chepe's relatives was a prime example. At first they were wary, and I confess that I was scared. I was treading dangerous ground far from home. But I soon relaxed as I told them my side of the story.

Ana, one of his sisters, nodded again and again as I poured out the details of Chepe's five trips to our house. I hadn't planned to tell them so much. But the living room full of people seemed ready to hear. As I told them how we loved Chepe and prayed for him, Ana started crying.

"Everything you say is true," she nodded through her tears. "Because when Chepe got drunk, his tongue loosened, and he would tell me all about the gringo he robbed again and again. Laughing, he would tell how he made you get on your bellies and how he would order you around. But he also told me several times, 'They are good people. They were kind to me and gave me food. And they told me about Jesus.' "

By then my heart was almost bursting.

Suddenly Ana got up and disappeared into the bedroom. She returned, holding a large picture frame almost reverently. Then she sat down, turned the photo toward me, and held it to her breast.

A surge of emotion flooded my being like a ten-foot breaker on some lonely beach. The face on the photo brought back so many memories, and most of them weren't sweet. I saw the long scar across his high cheekbone, his long brown hair, and especially those eyes. I had always said that if I ever saw those big brown eyes again, I would recognize them on the spot. And I did.

Then it was my turn to cry.

Clutching the picture frame, Ana sobbed, "I was the only person who really loved him."

Chepe's father squirmed in his seat. He knew it was true. He had learned to hate his delinquent offspring.

"I would always feed him," Ana continued. "I would take time to talk to him. I thought I was the only person in the world who loved him."

Though she didn't say it, her face and tears told the story. She was blessed to discover other people who loved him also—loved him enough to pray for him and to wish him the best. And I was blessed to know I was in that number.

I prayed for the family. They gave me permission to use Chepe's story for this book as long as I changed his name. By the time we parted, we had bonded, and Chepe's relatives were my friends. I knew the love of Jesus had touched their hearts. And instead of wanting to shoot me for hunting out their family secrets, they would rather have hugged me. And that gave me much peace.

———————

Franklin's relatives were ready to talk too. As professing Christians, they seemed to want to get the story out, as if freeing their own consciences. Having a robber in the family is a shameful thing in Nicaragua.

When we discussed the fact that he was skinned alive, his uncle hesitated. It just seemed too gross to talk about. But then his wife, up till then just listening, started talking. She told of the two areas of his body that were skinned. At the end of the interview, she gave the last, horrible tidbit of the story. "They cut out his tongue . . ."

After Franklin was killed, Manuel, the only one in the family who knew of the trap he had set, fell sick of guilt and remorse. Eventually he confided in his dad and brothers, telling them about the trap. In time, Franklin's relatives from far and near found out the truth. Guilty and reproached by all, Manuel finally took his own life by drinking pure herbicide.

Several years after Franklin died, Santiago's sons also caught Rigo, the ruffian who accompanied Franklin to kill the two men. He was also tortured brutally before they cut off his head.

––––––––––––

When I interviewed Roberto's father, Don Pancho, he was more than ready to frankly share Roberto's story. It was a joy to hear Don Pancho's own testimony, how he left the dark world of drink and superstition, finding freedom in Christ.

"This book would be an excellent tool to keep more young people from heading down the devil's broad lane," Don Pancho agreed. "Maybe this clear warning will help save a few."

After Roberto's death, Pedro kept moving closer and closer to Kusulí, trying to get back home. Old Pancho had no intention of avenging his son's death, either through bloodshed or prosecution, and the police chose to let the matter lie. Some had actually cheered Roberto's death.

Alfredo failed to learn from his brother's example. He left the area and continued his life of wickedness.

––––––––––––

Fausto and Paco's stories were the easiest part of my research for this book. And the most enjoyable. That's because I had a firsthand eyewitness. Once Fausto understood that I had forgiven him and that he was safe with me, the stories just poured out. It was such an eye-opener into a robber's life to hear him explain what happened and how he and Paco felt during the two robberies at our place and during his other experiences.

I can say that researching Fausto's story was a real thrill. My youngest son, Kenny, and I traveled way back to Casca and spent a day and night with Fausto and his family. They treated us like kings, and we almost got sick eating so much chicken soup, which is their best dish. It was delicious!

During the night, tossing and swinging on my hammock, I thought of what an easy trap they could have set for me. Vicente and another converted brother of his were along too. All three had been big-time robbers. I was way back in the boonies where a kidnapping would have been peanuts. But I smiled as I tried to find sleep in my cocoon. And as I prayed for the dear man and his family, I knew I was in no danger at all. I was as safe with them as I would have been with a threesome of Amish men!

I admit that I have mixed feelings about Fausto's spiritual life. I believe that God has begun a work in his heart, but I also realize it's not finished. As I learn to know him more, I realize he has a long way to go. For example, he has not been totally honest with his wife. She doesn't know that he stole from us. She knows he was a robber and kidnapper, but she doesn't know half of the things he has done in his past. I encouraged him to tell her everything. He promised to tell her at some later date.

The other thing Fausto and his brothers are facing is restitution. He seemed bold and willing to open up his life, but when I encouraged him to make full restitution to the others he'd wronged, he wavered. "Maybe someday," was his answer.

All we can do is ask the Lord to finish His work in Fausto's heart. That's where you, dear reader, can get involved. As God reminds you, pray for Fausto and his precious family.

Christ gave His life on the cross voluntarily that Fausto could be forgiven and live eternally. And now Fausto's reasonable service is to put his whole life on the altar. His willingness to tell his story for this book is a step in that direction.

INTRODUCTION

It was dark as we climbed the hill that night and approached the wooden, two-story house, masked and ready. My buddy carried a machete. I carried a machete and a knife. Though we were nervous, we were determined to hold up the *gringo*[1] (American) missionaries and steal their money.

We did get a bunch of money that night, though my fellow robber never gave me much of it. But I discovered that stealing from the *gringos* was easy. They didn't resist us. They were friendly and offered us food. Sure, we had to listen to their sermons and their pleas that we change our ways and seek God. But that seemed a cheap price to pay for a good night's haul.

"That was peanuts," I told my buddies many times. "And almost fun!"

I went back later to steal again, and again—five times in all. I was as punctual as a cuckoo clock, assaulting them at seven o'clock in the evening.

There were three missionary houses, all perched on separate hills. Through the grapevine I've heard that I wasn't the only robber to climb those hills. Many other men climbed them under cover of darkness, coming in from every direction—east,

1 *Spanish words and their pronunciations are listed at the back of the book.*

west, south, and north. We all had one thing in common: we wanted the *gringos'* money. And if they didn't have any money, we took their things.

Sometimes there were lone robbers. Sometimes they came by twos, like the time I went with my buddy. Several times there were three, and at least once there were four. One night a group of ten well-armed men climbed the hill in the moonlight. Then one fateful morning, a lone robber, drunk and crazed, climbed the hill at four o'clock in the morning and held them up with a machete and a green banana which he pretended was a pistol.

These and many other stories circled the hills of Waslala, and I heard them. I knew they were true. At least forty of us climbed those three hills between 1996 and 2000 and robbed the three missionary families. We always thought of what we could get from them. We tried to block from our minds the suffering they went through. We really didn't care, as long as we had money to buy our drugs and drink.

The years ticked by, and we never knew that the missionaries were praying desperately for grace to forgive us, for love to continue serving us, and for opportunities to witness to us. They even prayed they might come in contact with us by day to show us more of God's love.

I never knew, back then, that the missionaries walked through the town of Waslala searching for our faces. A thousand times they searched the streets, the buses, even out in the country, always asking themselves, "Could this be one of our robbers?"

Why did those missionaries act so strangely, when the other people we robbed were always so full of fear, panic, and hatred? What made them so different?

I didn't know then, but I do now. There is a verse in the Bible where Jesus says, "But I say unto you which hear, love your enemies, do good to them which hate you, bless them that

curse you, and pray for them which despitefully use you . . .
and your reward shall be great, and ye shall be the children of
the Highest: for He is kind unto the unthankful and to the evil
. . ." (Luke 6:27, 28, 35).

Back then I didn't often take the time to think about truth. I
blocked God from my heart and mind. I didn't realize how He
felt about me. I was one of God's lost sons, working in darkness. When God looked down and saw us wicked men, running around in the dark doing evil, He pitied us. We were His
lost children. He loved us and longed for our salvation. But
since we didn't heed His call, He chose to use unique ways to
touch our lives with His love. Sometimes He chose to use His
missionary children to be His hands to touch our wicked lives.

God gave those missionaries grace to love us, their robbers.
No, it was not easy for them. I see it all clearly now. Of course,
they struggled again and again and had to beg God for love
for us when we harassed them. Although we never guessed
it, they sometimes got angry. No, they didn't love us with a
friendly, brotherly love. They loved us with divine *agape* love.
God gave them the grace to love us enough to forgive us, to
give us food and drink; to joyfully allow the spoiling of their
goods. He gave them a love big enough to pray for us daily.
And, though we hated to admit it, we felt those prayers. I understand now that they never asked that we, the robbers, be
punished. They prayed for our salvation. God used that love
to give us countless opportunities. Some of us rejected that
love. Others accepted it.

Over the years God allowed the missionaries to discover our
stories so that Pablo could write this book to warn you, my
friend. If you are rejecting God's love, remember, it's a very
costly love. Stop rejecting His love today, because today is the
day of salvation.

"God is just: He will pay back trouble to those who trouble you and give relief to you who are troubled. . . . This will happen when the Lord Jesus is revealed from heaven in blazing fire with His powerful angels. He will punish those who do not know God and do not obey the gospel of our Lord Jesus. They will be punished with everlasting destruction" (2 Thessalonians 1:6-9, NIV).

God's love is a costly love. It cost Him the shed blood of His only begotten Son, Jesus. That's why I am trying to wake up your heart, my friend. Please listen! It's not worth it. The price of rejecting Him is very high. It often leads to death, and that's no joke in itself. Then it's hell for all eternity. And no one can tell you better than I can that it's awful down here!

Believe me, I know what I am talking about!

How do I know this so well? Perhaps I should start at the beginning.

My name is Chepe Rodríguez[2] . . .

---

2 *Names are changed throughout the book to protect their identity.*

Chapter One

A LIFE GONE AWRY

The Kusulí night was very dark. Even so, several cicadas whined on the laurel tree that pierced the inky sky above the two men. The evening heat was typical for the height of the Waslala dry season. The date was April 25, 1996. The time was eight o'clock.[3]

"Listen; they are singing," the taller robber, called Douglas, whispered as he pulled his bill cap lower over his face.

The short robber, called Chepe, nodded. "I bet they are having church."

"Why would the gringos be having church in their house?" Douglas asked quietly, crouching behind the fence that served as their hideout. "Don't they have a church house?"

"No," Chepe answered. "They are new in the area. I think they rent a house in town for their services. Maybe we shouldn't bother them tonight if they are having church."

"Bah, church or no church," Douglas bragged, "we will take their dollars tonight. Gringos always have money, and we will make them hand it over before the hour is up."

---

3 *The missionaries' side of this story can be found in* Angels Over Waslala, *chapter 27.*

Chepe nodded vigorously and added, "And we'll give them the scare of their lives, won't we?"

"Are you sure they don't carry guns?" Douglas wondered, craning his neck, trying to get a glimpse of what might be happening inside the large wooden building that loomed high on the hilltop in the darkness.

"No, they are very friendly and don't carry arms, but we will still need to be careful." Chepe reached down and swatted at some pesky ants crawling up his tattered blue pants. "We have to be ready for anything."

"Well, what are we waiting on then?" Douglas hissed. "They're still singing. Hey, let's smoke some pot yet before we hit."

They smoked their own rolled cigars, lost in their own thoughts. *Since we don't have real guns,* Douglas mused, *we will have to be rough so they get scared. Who knows how many there are? They might try some trick on us. I am going to have to be the leader, because this pipsqueak has so little brains that the gringos could easily catch him and take him to Waslala and stick him in jail. He's way too soft. He wanted to wait for another night because they are having a service. What a sissy!*

Chepe's thoughts were of a different nature. *I wonder what the gringos will be like. I have seen them in Waslala at times, but I have never talked to them. I have to be careful, too, or Douglas will take all the money and leave me as broke as I was before tonight. Douglas is such a mean, loud-mouthed bragger. But I guess that makes a good robber.*

The men smoked in silence. Douglas was dark-skinned, tall, and thin with short-cropped black hair. Chepe was short and skinny with long, almost wavy chestnut hair and a scraggly beard. They both wore poor *campesino* (peasant) clothes and looked as if they hadn't had any money in a long time—just enough to buy marijuana. Since they often didn't even have that, they stole to support their vice.

The house on the hilltop was quiet now. The lower story windows and doors were open and yellow light streamed from them, making the dark house look as if it had eyes staring down at the two men. The upstairs windows were closed and dark. The generator out in the *rancho* (thatched-roof shack) roared.

"Well, are you ready?" Douglas whispered as he tied his hanky over the lower part of his face.

Chepe nodded, following suit.

"Do you have your ammunition?" Douglas chuckled as he checked Chepe's weapons: a big machete, a knife in his belt, and a fake hand grenade. "I have my gear," he added, patting the knife in his own belt and cradling the big machete in his hands like a gun. "Tonight, this is my machine gun!"

The two men crawled through the fence. "We will run up the hill quietly. I will take that window," Douglas pointed. "You come in the front door at the same time. I will then tell you what to do, okay?"

Chepe nodded.

"Are you scared?" Douglas hissed. "Just pretend you're back in the army during the war. When I holler, 'Attack!' we take that house and the loot is ours. Ready?"

Chepe found himself trembling. He sensed that Douglas was also afraid. They stood at the foot of the hill as if frozen. Both men had been involved in robberies before, but it was always nerve-racking to get started. There was no way of knowing what they might face. Sometimes the people panicked. Sometimes they got angry and fought back. Sometimes they pulled out guns. That's just how things were in Nicaragua. It was a risk they had to take.

Chepe swallowed. His mouth was powder-dry. He licked his lips and looked at Douglas again, crouched and ready to run. Then finally Douglas squeaked out the command: "Attack!"

They both broke into a run as they climbed the steep lawn and ambushed the *gringo's* house.

Chepe played it safe. Instead of running up to the door and letting himself be seen, as he was supposed to, he skirted the house and stayed back far enough that he could see what was going on, yet be out of danger. From his vantage point, he could see Douglas and the group of people in the living room.

Chepe almost laughed when he saw that Douglas had chickened out, too. Instead of standing right in the window, he landed just to one side of the window where he felt a little safer. Unfortunately, there was a stack of tin under the window on which they were drying a pile of corn. Since the tin was slippery, the dry ears did not make good footing, and Douglas appeared to dance a jig as he tried to gain his footing. All the while, he was banging at the open shutter, hollering in a muffled voice through his hanky, "*Bo-a-bao! Bo-a-bao!* (face down)"

Looking into the window, Chepe saw the *gringos* for the first time that night. They were sitting around in a circle, still in the middle of their service. His heart turned cold when he saw that there were a whole bunch of them, men and women mixed. The ladies all wore white scarves on their heads and the men were all neatly dressed. For some reason, he suspected that the rumors were true: these people would not fight back.

As soon as they heard the noise at the window, the *gringos* fell silent, their faces stricken with fear. A lean, middle-aged *gringo* jumped up and stared out the window, pointing at Douglas, his eyes bulging. A chubby *gringo* jumped up from his chair and tried to peer around the corner. Chepe could see that they were confused and did not understand Douglas's insistent "*Bo-a-bao!*" The chubby *gringo* hissed to his companion, "That guy must be crazy!"

A German shepherd raced out from behind the house and barked angrily at Chepe. But she kept her distance, and Chepe right away saw that she wouldn't bite him.

A tall, blond young man immediately understood what was happening. He had raised his arms in surrender from the start. When he realized that the others didn't know what was going on, he said quietly, "That man is yelling, *'Boca abajo.'* "

The chubby *gringo* looked over the group and announced, "Let's all get down." And they did. Fast. Suddenly, everyone in the room understood—this was a robbery.

Douglas jumped over to the window and hunched down so that only his masked face could be seen by the *gringos* on the floor. He cradled his machete in his arms professionally, as if it were a machine gun. Chepe sprinted over to the door, knowing that Douglas would want quick action. There would be trouble if he didn't show up. He peered in the door. The floor was completely covered with prostrate forms. *The gringos sure are being obedient tonight,* he thought.

Douglas was in control now. "Someone go cut that generator off. Quick!" he snapped.

The chubby man got up from the floor slowly. Stepping over the prostrate forms, he carefully walked toward the door, straight toward Chepe. Chepe steeled himself.

Douglas looked at Chepe, and his scream pierced the night again. "Hey, you! Go with him and don't let him try any tricks!"

The chubby *gringo* met Chepe face-to-face and wordlessly motioned him to follow. Chepe could see that he was nervous, but nothing like the men of the house usually were in robberies like this.

As they approached the *rancho,* the *gringo* motioned to Chepe to wait outside while he took a second to slip inside. Before the generator's voice was silenced, the *gringo* was back out, standing beside Chepe. The generator stopped, the inverter kicked in, and though the lights blinked, they kept right on shining.

As they walked back toward the house, the *gringo* motioned to Chepe to come closer. "Look," he whispered. "Please be *tranquilo* (calm). You don't have to be afraid of us. We will cooperate and give you all the money we have."

"Do you have guns?" Chepe blurted out the question.

"Oh, no. We don't carry arms. Just relax; we will not hurt you." Then, hearing Douglas's shrill voice yelling at someone to shut up the dog, Chepe followed the *gringo* back to the house.

The chubby *gringo* hissed at the dog, then reentered the house. Chepe followed. A little girl with curly, blond hair was crying softly on the floor with the rest. The mother was patting her, trying to calm her fears. "Shut that little girl up!" Douglas screamed.

"I want all your money," Douglas raved. "Fast! All your billfolds and cash! No tricks!" Then, motioning to the chubby *gringo*, he barked, "You collect it."

The *gringo* reached into his hip pocket and pulled out his wallet. He tried to extract only the money, but Douglas yelled at him, "No, sir! Hand over the whole thing! Quick!"

Chepe soon learned that the chubby *gringo* was called Pablo. All the fellows on the floor either handed their money over to Pablo or told him where to find it. Several times Chepe had to follow Pablo upstairs for money stashed away in their bedrooms.

On their first trip up the stairs, Pablo led the way. Chepe was right behind him. When they reached the landing at the top, they found three wide-eyed children were standing in the doorway of one of the bedrooms. Looking past Pablo, Chepe saw the three children hand some money to him, and they quickly exchanged some words. Then they ran back into their room and lay down on the bed. Pablo entered another room to locate another person's money.

After all the money had been collected, Douglas started asking for things that would sell for quick cash. Soon he had a camera. As Chepe and Pablo looked through the kitchen cabinets, around the corner from Douglas, Chepe noticed a cake. It looked awfully good, and Chepe was starving. He was shocked when Pablo asked, "Hey, are you hungry? I would gladly give you this cake."

"Do you have pop?" Chepe asked as he accepted the pan.

"I'm sorry. We don't have pop, but let me gather some food for you."

"Yeah," Chepe answered as they strode back into the living room.

"I'll find a bag to put it in," Pablo assured him, steering toward the back porch to find a bag. Chepe could hardly wait to sink his teeth into that delicious cake. *Douglas and I will have a real party on the way home tonight,* he gloated.

But Douglas was furious when he saw the cake. He swore and cursed at his partner, "We are not a bunch of starving thieves! Give that junk back and help me get the dollars. We want lots of dollars tonight. Where are they? We know you are planning to buy a farm. Where is the money?"

Chepe laid the cake pan aside, embarrassed at his buddy's heartlessness. *These guys are being so nice,* he thought, his anger building. *Why can't he be a little nicer, too?*

Pablo made his way over the bodies toward Douglas, Chepe following. As they stepped over the lady with the little girl, Chepe could hardly believe his ears. The lady was still patting her and humming to her softly. *Wow,* Chepe mused, *no mother I know would be humming to her baby in this kind of situation.*

Pablo faced Douglas at the window. Douglas drew back in fear. Chepe almost smiled when he heard him snap, "Don't you dare hit me!"

"I'm not going to hit you," Pablo assured him. "I just came to talk to you. Relax. We are Christians and we won't hurt you. We just don't have much money on us. The reason you got so much tonight is because we have visitors."

"Well, let's see how much we have," Douglas suggested, a little calmer now. "You count it."

Chepe produced what the *gringo* had been giving to him during the raid. But he kept a stash in one of his pockets, just in case Douglas didn't cooperate later.

Pablo's hands were trembling like a leaf in the wind as he organized the money and tried to count it. "Are you afraid?" Douglas taunted. "Cut out the fear, man. Be quicker. Hurry!"

There was not much money in the pile on the windowsill. Chepe could see that this frightened the *gringo*. It made Douglas angry. "Where is all the money?" he shouted. Then he made Pablo ask all the men how much they had given. Sure enough, there was a bunch of money missing.

Chepe knew he would hear it from Douglas later. But for the moment Douglas focused his anger on a tall *gringo* who didn't seem to know how much he had given. He threatened to blow his brains out, and finally the *gringo* confessed that he still had $600 in the vehicle.

Douglas made Pablo lie down on his stomach, then he sent Chepe and the tall man out to the vehicle to get the money, which was slyly hidden behind a metal plate on the car door. The *gringo* had to use a wrench to loosen some bolts to get it out. *He wasn't able to trick us tonight!* Chepe gloated.

The tall *gringo* took the money to Pablo. Pablo got up and took it to Douglas, counting it out to him. It was the full $600.

After more threatening and shouting, Douglas was suddenly ready to leave. He shot a furious look at Pablo. "If you tell the police about this, I will hunt you down and kill you!"

Pablo promised not to tell the authorities for twenty-four hours. *That's plenty of time for us to be safely back in Waslala,* Chepe thought, relieved.

Douglas suddenly tried to be nice. "I didn't hurt your little girl, did I?" he asked quietly.

"No, you didn't," Pablo answered. "I appreciate that you didn't hurt us."

"Get back down on the floor!" Douglas snapped.

Pablo lay down among his friends.

"*Feliz noche* (happy night)," Douglas said sweetly as he backed away from the window. Chepe didn't say a word. He evacuated the house and walked around the corner to meet Douglas. Then Chepe and his buddy had the surprise of their life. In response to Douglas's parting words, several of the *gringos* hollered out, "May God bless you!"

The two robbers were silent as they hurried out the lane, their minds churning. They both knew that the evening's deal wasn't over. They had to settle, and they both dreaded it.

Once they hit the main road, walking fast toward Waslala, Chepe started the conversation. "Strange people, aren't they?" he said, hoping Douglas wouldn't remember the missing money.

"Humph, strange people, right! And you are a strange robber," Douglas growled, stopping in the middle of the road, blocking Chepe's way. "You dish that money out right now. I should have known you are a low-down, stinking skunk. You have at least $400 on you somewhere. Hand it over right now before I knock your teeth out."

"I'm getting a share too," Chepe whined. "I helped steal it!"

"Of course you'll get your share. But that's when we settle. First, we get it all together, and then we count it and divide it out. You know the rules. Hand it over!"

"Will you give me half?" Chepe whispered, shaking in fear.

"I said you'll get your share," Douglas snapped, raising his machete high. "Give me that money now!"

Chepe cowered under the machete. He knew good and well that if he handed the money over, he might never get his share. But he also knew that if he didn't, he would have to fight Douglas on the spot, and he was not ready for that. Douglas was too smart and too strong for him. So, digging through his hip pockets, he found the wad he had planned to keep for himself and gave it to Douglas.

Douglas turned on his heel and started walking toward Waslala again.

"What about my share?" Chepe stuttered.

"You'll get that in due time. Right now, we head for Waslala as fast as we can."

As they walked for the next hour and a half, Chepe had a lot of time to think. Douglas was gloating over their good hit and what he would do with so much money. Chepe was wishing he had stolen from the *gringos* alone. It really wasn't hard, since they were so cooperative. Then he would have had all that money for himself.

But as he thought it over, he began to feel cheap for hurting such nice people. *Why were those people so nice to us, even though we scared them badly? It must be because they are Christians, like Pablo said. Man, Douglas sure didn't care if they were nice or not. He hammered away at them as if they were animals. Those poor ladies and children were surely frightened to death. I wonder what they're doing now. If I ever steal from them again, I'll be nicer to them.*

Memories flooded Chepe's mind as he walked. As a young boy, he had been hyperactive and rambunctious. Everyone soon tired of his wild antics. He could never hold still or be good. He became unmanageable, disobedient, and bitter. By the time he became an adolescent, his parents had given up on him, and he was on his own.

Most of the family was happy when I got hurt climbing that tangerine tree when I was twelve, he thought. *As I slid down the trunk, my lip got hooked on that huge thorn. When my brother came to unhook me, the gash on my lip was awful. My dad wanted to whip me for it, but my sister Ana stood between us. She said the gash was punishment enough.*

Chepe rubbed the inch-and-a-half-long scar extending from his lip upward to his cheek. The scar had become a symbol of the lack of love in his childhood. By the time Chepe finished adolescence, the only person who loved him was his sister, Ana. The rest of the family despised him. So he joined the army.

Right now he missed Ana. She lived in faraway El Cuá with the rest of his family.

The two robbers arrived at Waslala around midnight. The streets were empty. Under a streetlight, Douglas told Chepe, "Look, you louse, I was the leader in this robbery. Even if it was your idea, I was the only one who could pull it off. You would never hurt a flea. You don't deserve half of the loot. I will give you this," he announced, handing him several hundred córdoba bills. "You'd better be glad I gave you anything at all."

Chepe's chest heaved as he thought of how it would feel to strike Douglas with his machete. But he knew he didn't stand a chance. All he could do was swallow, take the few bills, and leave. He did manage to choke out, "I will never go with you again!" as he turned and fled.

As he retreated, he heard Douglas sass back, "And I will never ask you again!"

The next week was hard on Chepe. Waslala was having a full-fledged fiesta. Chepe went to the fiesta the day after the robbery. He met Douglas at the bull-riding event, dressed in brand-new clothes—expensive blue jeans, cowboy boots, and a new checkered shirt. He was laughing with his friends and buying beer as if he had all the money in the world. Chepe heard one of his buddies tell a friend, "It's strange. Douglas is walking around with dollars. Nobody in Waslala carries dollars."

Chepe stewed over his loss. And every day he stewed, the new idea that had hatched in his mind grew stronger. *I will go to the gringos again. But this time I will go alone.*

The date was May 9, 1996. Chepe was smoking his marijuana alone this time. He stood in a chest-high stand of grass and leaned against another laurel tree. Two weeks ago, he and Douglas had ambushed the *gringos'* house from below. This time Chepe was alone and planned to ambush from above, from the knoll behind the house. [4]

Chepe had chosen the spot at dusk, just when he could still see. He had watched for an hour. He was sure the *gringos* were alone and no neighbors were around to cause any trouble. He was almost ready to roll, but he needed that last puff to give him courage.

As Chepe smoked, he chuckled. Earlier, he had painstakingly cut an oval from the center of a four-by-four-foot sheet of black plastic. He had cut out holes for his eyes, nose, and mouth. Then he had made tiny holes at each end of the piece and tied a string to one end that he would wrap around his head once he was ready.

Plastic Hood and Mask

---

4 *The missionaries' side of this story can be found in* Angels Over Waslala, *chapter 28.*

Now, ready for action, Chepe took the remaining sheet of plastic and stripped it over his head like a cape. Carefully he tied the mask. *This will make the gringos tremble,* he bragged to himself. Then he checked his armor. He had his ever-present machete and a sharp knife stuck in his belt. He was ready to go.

Overcoming the natural fear he felt whenever he robbed a house, he walked down the hill at a good clip. It was seven o'clock. The house seemed quiet as the robber snuck around the side that was closed up and dark. The dog didn't detect his arrival. He went straight for the window Douglas had worked from two weeks earlier. Stepping up to the window, his right hand under the cape as though he carried a pistol, he said in a commanding voice, "*¡Boca abajo todos!*" (Everybody face down!)

He felt a strange satisfaction as he watched the blood drain from the people's faces, and they hit the cement floor in a flash. He was boss. He had power.

There weren't nearly as many *gringos* at home this time, but even so, Chepe quickly counted nine bodies strewn in different positions in the living and dining room. "Go get the radio," he commanded. "I know you have a radio to communicate."

The pudgy man Chepe knew as Pablo raised his head from the cold cement floor and asked in a quiet voice, "Shall I go alone, or do you want to go with me?"

"Go alone, quick!"

It took Pablo a long time to unhook the radio, and Chepe paced the porch nervously. He banged on the next window along the side porch, but Pablo didn't open it. When he came out with the radio, instead of taking it from him, Chepe barked, "Just tear up some wires on the thing!"

"But why?" Pablo asked.

"Cause I know that, after I leave, you'll call the police," Chepe growled.

"Oh, no," Pablo explained. "This CB radio is only for close contacts. Actually, the only people I can call are the ones from right around here."

"Okay, lay it aside," Chepe answered, relieved.

While Pablo worked on the radio, Chepe told a tall, blond young man that he needed money.

"We don't have much," the *chele* (pale-faced one) explained. "We were just robbed two weeks ago, and there's not much money left."

"Who came?" Chepe wanted to know.

"We don't know," the *chele* replied, "but they took quite a bit of money."

"What else did they take?" Chepe asked.

The young man on the floor obediently answered all his questions. Feeling a touch of pity toward the poor, frightened people who lay stretched out on the floor, Chepe added, "Look, I am not planning to hurt you. I just need money. Dollars, I want lots of dollars."

Pablo brought all the money they had in the house. It wasn't much. "Hey," Chepe commanded, his voice rising, "you have more money than this. Get it quickly!"

Pablo patiently explained again. "We were just robbed two weeks ago. We don't have much money. We are Christians, and we don't lie. If you don't believe me, search the house."

Chepe shook his head. For some strange reason, he did with the *gringos* what he never did with anybody else—he believed them. He just knew that what they said was true.

"Bring me a recorder," he demanded.

In no time Pablo was back with a small, red tape player. Just before handing the tape player over to Chepe, he opened the thing and pulled out a tape. "No," Chepe commanded. "Leave the tape in it."

"Look," Pablo countered, "this tape is a family favorite. Besides, you won't understand it. I will get you a Spanish one."

Chepe agreed.

Chepe entered the house to see what else he could take. He motioned toward the kitchen and then followed Pablo, his eyes darting through the holes in the black mask. To his surprise, he saw Pablo getting cheese out of the refrigerator, from which he cut off a generous chunk. Then he grabbed a loaf of bread and stuffed the food into a plastic bag and handed it to him. Chepe was awfully hungry and grabbed the bag eagerly. Then he asked, "You don't have any pop, do you?"

Pablo jerked around and looked at the robber. Chepe remembered that he had asked for pop two weeks ago. But Pablo answered just like he had the other time. "No, we don't have pop."

Changing the subject, Chepe snapped, "I want five pairs of boots."

Pablo stepped out onto the back porch and began gathering the family's collection of rubber boots. But Chepe complained, "No, I don't want rubber boots. I want leather boots. Good boots."

Pablo handed him his good leather tie shoes. Next it was the watches. Then, "Let's go over to the other *gringo's* house to get his money." Turning to the prostrate group, he ordered, "You all stay lying flat until we come back. My buddies outside will be watching your every move."

"Couldn't they at least sit up and relax?" Pablo pleaded.

"Okay, they can get up, but hold still and don't make any noise. Let's go!" he ordered.

The night was dark, and a gentle rain had started to fall. As they walked down the hill, Chepe wondered at the pudgy man ahead of him. For some reason, the man wasn't scared of him anymore.

As they passed the small cement building at the base of the hill, Chepe asked Pablo, "What's in there?"

"That's where we keep the medicine we give out to the poor people," Pablo answered.

"Stop," Chepe said. "I want to take some medicine tonight."

Pablo ran back up to the house to get the keys. Soon he returned and unlocked the small building. He pulled out all kinds of medicines and packed them into Chepe's bag. But the bag filled up too quickly. So Pablo suggested, "I will get a larger bag at Tim's place, and we will stop for the rest of the stuff you need on the way back."

After exiting the building, Chepe said, "Go by yourself to the other man's house. I will wait here. Bring all his money."

Fifteen minutes later Pablo was back, puffing but smiling. He apologized that Tim had only fifty-one córdobas ($5) on him. Chepe didn't complain. Then Pablo opened the cement house again and began repacking all the things Chepe had acquired. He added more medicine and then placed the cheese on top of the bag. Patting the bag gently, Pablo said, "Here is your bread and cheese, right on top. Remember, that's just for you!"

"*¡Gracias!* (Thanks!)" Chepe answered sincerely.

As soon as they left the building, Chepe asked, "You have a *lapa* (macaw), don't you?"

"Yes," Pablo admitted.

"Go get it," Chepe demanded.

"Sure," Pablo answered and then sprinted up the hill one more time. As he left, Chepe yelled at him, "Tell my buddies to meet me out by the road. I am just about ready to go."

Minutes later Chepe grinned to himself as he heard Pablo holler into the rainy darkness, "Friends, your comrade wants you to go meet him out by the road."

Does Pablo actually believe there are other men out there, or is he just playing along with my game? Chepe wondered.

When Pablo returned with the *lapa* perched on his arm, Chepe was frightened. The big, red bird had a huge, menacing beak.

"Does she bite?" he asked quickly.

"No, she is as tame as a kitten. She is our favorite pet," Pablo explained as he held the *lapa* close to his face, occasionally whispering in her ear, *"Adios, lapita.* (Goodbye, little macaw.)"

Then Pablo handed over the *lapa.* Apprehensively, Chepe bared his thin arm from under the plastic. *"Lapita, lapita!"* she said gruffly as she stepped over onto his arm obediently.

Chepe was ready to leave. His backpack was crammed to the gills. The bag from Tim's house was also full, slung over his shoulder by its strap, and the *lapa* was perched on his arm. He was ready to go, yet he was in no hurry. He had been with this man for almost an hour, and he felt a strange attachment to him. Though common sense told him they were enemies, they didn't feel like enemies at all. Chepe just wasn't sure how to say goodbye to his new friend.

Pablo made the first move. The night was dark, and the steady drizzle had wet his face and hair. Through the gloom, Chepe could see that Pablo's face was sad, yet kind. Then Pablo did something so unheard of that Chepe was never able to forget it. He placed his hand on Chepe's shrouded shoulder and said, "Do you know what? I love you with the love of Jesus."

Chepe was speechless. He had never received much love in his life. As far as he knew, only his sister, Ana, loved him. Not even his own mother loved him anymore. Yet this strange man had treated him nicely all evening and now told him sincerely that he loved him. It hit a lonely spot in his heart, and tears welled in his eyes.

The minister continued. "I want you to know that my family and I will be praying for you every day. We will pray that God will touch your heart with the love of Jesus. Count on it, we are your friends."

Chepe's chest heaved with emotion. He held back the flood of tears that threatened to burst. He still didn't know what to say, yet he wanted to say something. At loss for words, he stood there as if waiting on something. Not even he knew what for.

Pablo had removed his hand from his shoulder. He was waiting, too. He put his hand on Chepe's shoulder again and whispered, "Goodnight." Then he turned to leave.

"Well, I didn't hurt you, did I?" Chepe asked, groping for words.

"That's right," Pablo agreed. "You weren't nearly as mean as the two fellows who came two weeks ago. We really appreciate that."

"I just want you to know that I don't want to hurt you," Chepe said in a pleading voice. "I just needed some money . . ."

"That's all right. We forgive you. Goodnight," Pablo repeated.

Chepe's "Goodnight" echoed Pablo's as he sprinted up the hill. Chepe walked out the lane slowly. The *lapa* kept repeating, in her funny gruff voice, *"Adios, adios."*

Chepe gave vent to his pent-up emotions by laughing. Shaking his head, he told the bird, "That sure is funny. I come here like an enemy and leave like a friend, almost crying. I wonder why." Suddenly he felt hot. He stopped, ripped off his mask and cape, and flung them down over a weedy bank. Then he started walking seriously toward Waslala. He had the next two hours to wonder what the *gringo* family was doing, and to ponder one of the strangest evenings in his stealing career.

Chepe's next two weeks were busy. He was staying with a brother-in-law's family right in town. They were a working family, so he stayed out of their way. They lived their lives, and he lived his.

Chepe kept the tape player for himself. He used the cash to buy drink and marijuana. It didn't take him long to find a buyer for the *lapa*. A rich farmer bought her, cheap.

However, it was the medicine which proved most valuable over time. Chepe became a peddler. He couldn't read or write, so he got Tirso, one of the boys, to read the labels on the bottles. He memorized them and went from house to house selling them. Chepe was a good salesman. He easily convinced the ladies of the house that they needed something for fever, parasites, fungus, or cough. Though Chepe sold the medicine at reasonable prices, he had plenty of it, and every day he made enough money to support his vice and to buy extra things for the family he stayed with.

The shoes were too big for him, so he sold them.

One day Efraín, another one of the boys, came home from cutting down trees in Kusulí. As soon as he'd had a cup of coffee, he told a story. Chepe was all ears.

"They kidnapped Don Lolo Lanza last evening," Efraín announced.

"Who did?" Chepe asked quickly.

"Nobody knows, but everybody believes it's the same group that's holding up passenger trucks on the main road. It's a big group, and they carry machine guns."

"Did they get any money out of him?" Chepe pressed.

"Yes, though nobody knows how much. Don Lolo made a deal with the robbers last night. They had him in the woods right across the road from the *gringos'* clinic. But they turned him loose when he promised not to involve the police and to meet them this morning with a huge amount of money. They say the robber who met him to receive the money was wearing Lolo's expensive watch that he had taken from him the night before. He met him at the Guabo Bridge in broad daylight."

"Why didn't Lolo take the police along and catch those robbers?" the lady of the house asked, eyeing Chepe.

"Don Lolo knows better," Efraín answered. "He knew they would have tracked him down and killed him. It was either the money or his life."

Chepe's eyes were shining. "I bet they got a lot of money."

"Waslala is getting bad," the lady of the house clucked. "When will the stealing and violence stop?"

Chepe grinned. "It might be a long time yet."

Two weeks passed quickly. The medicine ran out. All Chepe's cash was gone. He decided it was time for another stealing binge. His thoughts were many and varied as he set about making plans.

Where shall I go? he wondered. *I pity the gringos. I don't hurt them physically, but I know they suffer. And Pablo is so nice. I hate to bother him again. But it's just so much easier to go to the gringos. Anywhere else I could get shot, or they might sic dogs on me. They mentioned that they have another tape player, and they might have more money by now . . .*

Chepe's mind swung from one thought to another. Every time it swung toward Kusulí, his thought pendulum hung there in suspense. Finally, he made up his mind. He would go and pretend he was not the same man. He would try to be mean and rough like Douglas had been. Maybe, just maybe, they would have more money this time. If not, there was always a lot of other stuff to pick up.

The date was May 29, 1996, not quite three weeks from the last time Chepe had robbed the *gringos*. He decided not to wear a cape, but chose to wear a plastic mask much like the one he'd worn before. He carried his infamous machete, and this time he also carried a special weapon, a phony hand grenade. He picked it up in the cacao (the fruit from which chocolate is made) patch right behind his friend's house. Recalling details from his past war experience, he chose the cacao fruit carefully. *I need a cacao that has splotches on it. A little past ripe. Just about perfect*, he decided, as he jerked it off the tree. *This will scare the gringos!*[5]

When Chepe tiptoed around the corner of Pablo's house, he was surprised to see the tall, blond fellow sitting on a chair on the porch while one of the ladies gave him a haircut. Several of the children were out there with them. Through the window, he could see Pablo sitting at the table, writing something. Meeting the people sooner than he expected, he found himself saying gruffly, *"Buenas noches* (good evening)" instead of the usual *"Boca abajo."*

The greeting had the same effect. Everybody on the porch ran for the house and flung themselves to the floor. Chepe positioned himself at the same window and started to give orders. "Is everybody here?" he asked roughly.

"No," Pablo answered. "My wife's upstairs. May she just stay up there?"

"No," Chepe barked. "Everybody must come down and get *boca abajo.*"

Pablo left to get his wife. Once they came back, Chepe made him quiet the dog, which was barking ferociously at him. Pablo stepped out on the porch and grabbed the dog by the scruff of the neck. He hauled her in to the tall guy and said, "Eldon, hold her, please."

Eldon, not cooperating completely with Chepe, was sitting on the floor instead of lying down. He pulled the mutt down beside him, and she shut up.

---

5 *The missionaries' side of this story can be found in* Angels Over Waslala, *chapter 31.*

"I need five pairs of boots," Chepe demanded, just like he had done two weeks before.

"Hey, we don't have any more," Pablo answered. "You took them all the last time."

Chepe was startled. *Now they know it's me again!*

"I have never been here before," he claimed.

"Oh, yes, you were," Pablo said firmly. "We know it's you. This is your third time here."

"Well, bring me the money," Chepe sassed. "All of it!"

While Pablo went upstairs for the money, Chepe tried to act like Douglas. Pointing at Eldon, he demanded, "I want 200,000 córdobas ($25,000) tonight, or I am going to kidnap Pablo!"

"We don't have that kind of money," Eldon explained. "We've told you that before."

"Well, then I want 100,000 córdobas," Chepe complained.

When Pablo returned, Chepe told Eldon, "You go to the other man's house and get his money. And hurry!" Then, turning back to Pablo, he bluffed, "If you don't get money, I am going to take one of the ladies to the jungle!"

Next Chepe took their watches. Eldon came back with the report that Tim had given his last money to his hired man. Chepe was not happy. So far he had only gotten about 400 córdobas ($50), a couple of watches, and a pair of shoes. Also, Pablo and Eldon were obviously not afraid of him anymore. Pablo was standing, and Eldon sat on the floor. The ladies were still frightened, but he was losing his power over the men.

Abruptly, Pablo sat down on the floor beside Eldon. "Sir," he addressed Chepe seriously, "why don't you consider stopping this job you have. Do you realize how dangerous your job is?"

"*We* won't hurt you," Eldon reasoned along with Pablo, "but you know good and well that Charro is in the area, and if he could, he'd get you."

Chepe knew all about Charro, the top leader of the Recontras, a guerrilla group currently operating in the area. He also knew Charro's slogan concerning robbers: "I have no jail for them—only a graveyard."

"Plus, you have God to deal with," Pablo added.

Chepe listened to the kind words of his new friends. Lamely, he answered, "At least I don't hurt people."

"But you are still stealing, and God will punish you for it," Pablo replied.

While Eldon went on explaining why Chepe should change his life, Pablo got up and went to the office without asking for permission. Soon he came back with a new Bible. Handing it to Chepe, he said, "This book, *mi amigo* (my friend), will change your life. Will you read it?"

"Yes, I will," Chepe promised.

"And here," Pablo said kindly, offering a bag of freshly-baked cookies, "is something especially for you."

"Thank you," Chepe said sincerely, forgetting that he had intended to be more like Douglas during this robbery.

"I need two sets of clothes!" Chepe blurted.

Pablo left to get the clothes.

Remembering that Pablo had forgotten to give him a cassette for his new tape player the time before, Chepe demanded, "I want cassettes. I want a whole bunch."

Pablo brought him the Spanish one he had promised.

"I want more than this," Chepe insisted.

"But we only have one in Spanish," Pablo explained.

"I don't care if they are in English. I want a bunch!"

He took fifteen cassettes. Suddenly, Chepe seemed to be finished. He asked, almost kindly, "I didn't hurt anybody, did I?"

"No," Pablo answered slowly, eyeing the hand grenade. "At least not physically. We appreciate that a lot."

It was time to leave. Was there a hint of a grin on Pablo's face? Chepe wondered if he had detected that the hand grenade was a cacao fruit. Impulsively, Pablo stuck out his hand to speed up the departure. "*Buenas noches* (goodnight)," he said warmly.

Taking his hand and shaking it naturally, Chepe answered, "*Buenas noches.*" Then he turned and slipped into the darkness.

As Chepe walked down the hill toward the main road, he wondered about Charro's men. *I must be careful,* he concluded as he hiked toward Waslala, picking up his pace.

———

Chepe was drunk. He wobbled over to Efraín's house carrying the bright red recorder. He had the a cappella music on, turned up high. "How can you know someday you'll be a Christian? . . ." The Miller Four's quartet sounded nice to Chepe's ears, even if he didn't understand it. Plopping down on a chair in the kitchen, Chepe turned and looked at Efraín, who was sharpening his chain saw.

"Hey, do you like my music?" he hiccupped.

Efraín ignored him.

Chepe insisted, "Hey, I will sell you some of these cassettes. I love to hear these songs."

Efraín turned and looked squarely at Chepe. "That is not Nicaraguan music. Where do you get it?" he growled.

"It's *gringo* music," Chepe burped. "A guy gave me a whole stack of them. I think they're great."

"I have a notion you're stealing from the *gringos* in Kusulí." Efraín said, pointing at Chepe's face.

Carelessly, Chepe laughed. "Hic . . . yeah . . . I have been visiting the pastor. They are nice people . . . hic . . . hic . . . very cooperative!"

"How do you do it?" Efraín asked sternly.

"I just go . . . hic . . . and make them stick their little rears in the air, and then I help myself," Chepe guffawed, slapping his leg in delight. Then he took another swig from his bottle. He didn't notice that Efraín was angry.

"Look," Efraín snapped. "You are going to get killed for your meanness. Those *gringos* are here to help the poor and to preach, and you molest them. I would be ashamed! If Charro gets hold of you and cuts your throat, don't think I'll go to your burial. You are asking for trouble. Why don't you steal from the Nicaraguans, you chicken? You're scared. They won't lay on the floor *boca abajo;* they'll blow your brains out, and it would serve you right."

Chepe stared at Efraín dumbly. He didn't say a word.

Efraín continued bitterly. "Look, if you ever try to pull a trick on me, it won't be as easy as hitting the *gringos.*" Caressing his pistol in his belt for emphasis, he finished, "You steal from me, and *bang,* that's the last of you. Now get out of here!"

Chepe wobbled back to Efraín's parents' house, the tape player blaring, "I'm packed and ready for the one-way flight to Heaven. . . ."

———

Chepe had an awful hangover the next morning. Soon after he got up, he asked Tirso's mother for a cup of black coffee. Then he took his little red recorder and his machete and headed for La Poza de los Compas (The Soldier's Pool). He walked through the poor folks' section at the edge of town and headed down the hill toward the Waslala River.

At the river, he turned and walked several hundred yards upstream and around several bends. Arriving at the infamous La Poza de los Compas, he noticed the pool was swollen and red-brown from the recent rains. Chepe wasn't planning to swim anyway. He just wanted some time alone.

Nobody knew why it was called La Poza de los Compas, but everybody knew who met at that pool. Even the police knew. It was the hangout for all of the town's druggies, shoe-shiners, and loose women. It was early enough in the morning that Chepe didn't expect to meet anyone there. The gathering would start several hours later, when the sun was hot. By going early, Chepe knew he could have some time alone.

On the far side of the water stood a little grove of guaba trees. Chepe found his favorite tree and sat down at its base. From that position, he could see the pool and the trails that came from town. The only place he couldn't see as he slouched at the base of the tree was the weedy hillside behind him. The only people who would come from that direction were his buddies. So he felt safe sitting there, facing the world.

Chepe turned on his little tape player. He had put in his favorite tape, *Koinonía,* the only Spanish one the *gringo* had given him. He closed his eyes as he listened. "One day at a time, sweet Jesus, is all I'm asking from you . . ."

Chepe wondered about his future. He certainly didn't know what was going to happen to him! In a sense, he lived one day at time, too.

But Chepe did know about his past. He remembered how his two older brothers had taught him to steal years ago. Then he remembered how they were both killed when they were caught stealing. He felt fortunate he hadn't been with them the time they were gunned down like dogs.

After his brothers were killed, Chepe had stopped stealing for a while. He had joined the army and gotten in on the last several years of Nicaragua's civil war. But he'd grown tired of the discipline and deserted the army and returned to Waslala, where he started stealing again.

A few years passed and he felt disoriented and unmotivated. He hated manual labor. Slowly, he allowed his depression to pull him down into a life of bumming, drinking, and smoking marijuana. Traveling between his family in El Cuá and his brothers-in-law in Waslala, he lived only for his vices and stole to finance them.

Chepe was getting sleepy. Just before he dozed off, he thought a strange thought. At least it was a strange thought for a vagabond like him. He wondered how it would be to live like the missionaries in Kusulí. *I could never be a Christian,* he yawned. *I couldn't sing all those lovely songs about Jesus. It would be nice, but I could never stop smoking marijuana and drinking liquor. It would be good to do all the good things Pablo talks about. But it would be too hard for me, plus stealing beats working any day.*

Chepe fell asleep thinking about his past—his tape player playing softly.

Suddenly, Chepe heard a quiet rustle and awoke with a start. Someone was standing behind him, staring at him. He turned his head slowly. The man was light-skinned and had long, bushy hair and a full brown beard. He wasn't wearing a shirt, and on his upper arm he sported a huge tattoo of a curled snake lifting its head out of the center. Above the tattoo was the word "Cobra."

Cobra's real name was Freddy; he was one of Waslala's biggest drug dealers. Now he smiled at Chepe, certain that he would buy some drugs. Chepe sat up and smiled back at his buddy. *I have to trick him,* he thought. *I dare not let him know I am totally broke.*

"Hey, do you have any weed?" Chepe asked, now fully awake.

"Sure. How much do you want?" Cobra hunched down beside his friend.

"I didn't bring my money along," Chepe lied. "But if you get me some, I have the money at the house. I'll get it to you later."

Soon the two men were puffing away and making plans for the future.

It had been almost two weeks since Chepe had visited the *gringos*. Every day he thought about his empty pockets and considered the possibility of going back. Though he pitied the missionaries and felt ashamed when they were so nice to him, it was just too easy to refurnish his dwindling supply of loot.

One evening Chepe came back from his daily peddling. He had sold only one cassette and his last bottles of vitamins. It was not enough to pay for his marijuana. He would have to sell his red tape player, and he already knew who would buy it.

As he walked into the house, Tirso was waiting for him, agitated and looking almost afraid. He called Chepe out into the back lot and got to the point right away. "Look, bud, we haven't gotten you in trouble because my brother is married to your sister. We know you are stealing from the *gringos* who came to this country to do us good. You know we don't appreciate that."

"I haven't gone down there in two weeks," Chepe whined.

"Well, let me tell you why you won't be going back there ever! Last night the Recontra hit the Kusulí area. People claim their sole purpose was to kill the robbers who molest the *gringos*. They caught two robbers. One lived really close to the *gringos'* place. They were young squirts who were just starting to steal. The leaders got away."[6]

"What did they do with the boys?" Chepe croaked, his big brown eyes bulging.

"They tortured them. They tied them to an old jeep and dragged them around during that hard rain last night. Then they stabbed them, cut their tongues out, and cut their throats. If they'd been able to get a hold of you, they would have done the same to you. I am warning you: Stop your stealing if you know what's good for you. Especially stop stealing from the *gringos*. Once Charro decides to defend the *cheles*, the robbers had better run!"

---

6 *You can read the whole story in* Angels Over Waslala, *chapter 30.*

Chepe stood and stared at his friend. Tirso pointed at him and barked, "This is the last time I am warning you, bud. Listen, and maybe you will be safe. Steal again, and you are a dead man!"

That night Chepe found a friend who would pay for his *cañita* (cheap alcoholic drink). Everybody was talking about the killing the night before. "There was a sign hung from a tree right beside the boys' bodies," one drinker told his buddy. "The crude cardboard sign simply said, 'These boys were part of Ricardo's robber band. Cadejos did this!' I saw it with my own eyes."

"Everybody trembles when they hear the nickname Cadejos," another client affirmed. "He's a short, stocky, light-skinned Recontra whose heart is as cold as stone. He fought in the war. Some claim that he is worse than Charro himself."

"They had the two boys stretched across the road right close to the *gringos'* clinic," the eyewitness continued. "It was gruesome. You could still see the pools of blood where they had wallowed in their dying moments. They say that Cadejos is determined to kill all the robbers who molest the *gringos.*"

Chepe couldn't get drunk quickly enough.

Two weeks later, the uproar about the killing had died down. Chepe was faced with a tough decision. It was a month since he had been to visit the *cheles.* He was not getting enough money for his vices, and his thirst was growing. He knew he could go and try the *gringos* again, but several things bothered him. He was afraid of Charro, for one thing, and of a trap.

Maybe the missionaries have agreed with Charro to kill us robbers, he thought. *What will I do if the gringos aren't afraid of me anymore? What will I do if they refuse to cooperate?*

Shall I go? If I do, I'll have to be meaner. I'll have to change my tactics. I'll need a gun. I'll need to choose a different mask. I'll need to come from a different side of the house. I'll go one more time, and it will have to work . . .

Then Chepe found out that a vanload of *gringos* had driven through Waslala on their way toward Kusulí. That clinched the trip in Chepe's mind. He remembered how many dollars those *gringo* visitors had when he'd robbed them with Douglas.

_____

The date was June 30, 1996. Dusk had fallen over the mountainous Kusulí outback. Chepe was back in his spot on top of the hill in the middle of the grass patch, looking down on the two-story wooden house below him. The generator was already roaring in the *rancho*. Yellow light streamed from every open window downstairs.[7]

Chepe wanted to be sure the *gringos* wouldn't recognize him as the same robber, so he took an old sack and cut a hole for his head and his arms. Next, he stripped it tightly over his upper body. Taking one of his big hankies, he cut two holes for his eyes. Then he tied it tightly over his head. He reached into his pocket and fingered his pistol. *This will be the first time that I will ambush the gringos with a pistol,* he grinned to himself.

As Chepe smoked his last marijuana cigar before heading for the house, he wondered how the *gringos* were feeling. It had been a month since his last hold-up, thanks to the Recontra. It wasn't like he wasn't afraid tonight. He was, but not afraid enough to drop his plan. His desperation for money and drugs was just a notch stronger than his fear. So he threw the cigar stub in the grass and marched toward the house. It was seven o'clock.

This time, Chepe approached the house from a totally different direction. He came around the *rancho*. Standing behind the guacamaya tree, he was afraid. He could see the family moving around inside the house. Then, abruptly stepping out from behind the tree, he began stomping his feet and shouting, "*¡Boca abajo!*"

_____

7 *The missionaries' side of this story can be found in* Angels Over Waslala, *chapter 36.*

To his relief, everyone quickly hit the floor. Slipping into the carport, he stood in the window, between the jeep and the wall. Shouting loudly, he demanded, "Get me 20,000 ($2,500) córdobas or I will burn this house down!"

Pablo slowly got up from the floor and walked over to the window, handing over his money. "We don't have much money," he said, "but we will gladly give you what we have."

"You go over to your friend's place and bring his money, too," Chepe said, just like he always did.

Turning around, Pablo told Eldon, "Just go call Tim and tell him to bring his money over."

Chepe decided that was okay.

"Where are the visitors?" Chepe asked. "I know you have visitors."

"They left yesterday," Pablo explained.

Chepe was disappointed. There was not going to be much money after all. And it looked as if they recognized him again. They sure didn't seem very scared of him anymore. Looking at Pablo through his horrid red hankie, he whined, "The first time we came and you had visitors, I never got any of that money. That maniac took it all—"

Suddenly, the dog started barking down the lane. Chepe swung around, and for the first time, Pablo and Eldon saw his gun.

"Don't be afraid," Pablo said. "It's Tim coming with his money."

Chepe squinted to catch sight of the advancing man, his pistol ready. Sure enough, a tall man strode out of the shadows straight toward him. Chepe hollered out to him, "Go inside and get *boca abajo!*"

Tim didn't break his stride. He kept on walking toward Chepe with a big smile on his face.

"Go in and get *boca abajo* right now!" Chepe screamed, holding his pistol out in front of him, cradled in both hands, pointed straight at Tim. But Tim didn't stop.

Chepe was sweating now. Tim must have guessed that his pistol wasn't real. He was just opening his mouth to shout again when Tim stopped in front of him and stretched out his hand to shake his. *"Buenas noches,"* he greeted cheerfully.

Chepe felt himself turning red. He let loose of the pistol with his right hand, further exposing the fake gun, and shook Tim's hand. He knew he was sunk. The *gringos* weren't scared of him anymore. Especially not when he carried a pistol carved out of laurel wood.

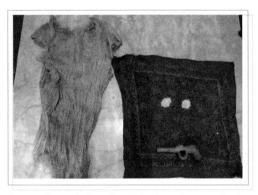

The hood, the mask, and the pistol—Chepe's gear during his fourth robbery.

After shaking his hand, Chepe ordered Tim to go inside and get *boca abajo*. He was worried, though, watching as Tim took his good old time, pulling off his dirty shoes and tiptoeing into the dining room. He saw Eldon sitting on the floor, and Pablo was standing.

"Get *boca abajo!*" Chepe hollered. But Tim just sat down on the floor beside Eldon.

Turning to Pablo, Chepe complained, "That guy doesn't obey me!"

"That's all right," Pablo assured him. "See, we know each other pretty good by now, don't we? You know we don't resist you or hurt you. We know how you operate. It's just not necessary anymore."

Then Pablo set to work getting some things ready for his friend, serving him as if Chepe were his best buddy. He put together a bag of cookies, a bag of popcorn, and the fried cheese sandwiches they were going to have for their evening meal. *They haven't eaten yet,* Chepe concluded as he watched Pablo pick the food off the table already set for his family. *They were just ready to start their meal.*

When Pablo approached Chepe to give him his gift, he also gave him all the money he'd been able to find. It wasn't much. About 200 córdobas ($25). Then Chepe asked for his watch. Pablo handed it over. *That's the third watch I have gotten from this man,* Chepe realized.

Not knowing what to do next, Chepe stood there, bags in hand, staring at the familiar scene. The ladies and children were strewn all over the floor, holding perfectly still. The men looked at him with their usual smiles. Chepe just didn't know what to do.

Tim thought of something to redeem the time. "Sir, have you ever thought about the danger you face when you come to steal from us? We don't tell the Recontra about you, but everybody finds it out. You must know how they killed two young men here two weeks ago."

Chepe nodded. "This work runs a certain risk. It's a risk I am willing to take."

"Plus, what about God?" Tim asked him seriously. "Someday God will say, 'That's enough!' Then what will you do?"

"We want to help you," Pablo threw in kindly. "We love you because Jesus teaches us to love our enemies. Why don't you change your lifestyle? If you would come here in the daytime, we could talk. I might even give you work, and you could make your own living and wouldn't have to steal."

Remembering something, Pablo disappeared into the little room where he kept his books. Soon he came out with a thin book and handed it to him. "This magazine is called *La Antor-cha de la Verdad*.[8] Read it, and it will help you find God."

Chepe took the book and pretended he could read as he paged through it. *What if these guys knew I can't read?* he pondered. He didn't know it, but they guessed as much, since he was reading with the magazine upside down.

Then Tim began to describe the plan of salvation. As he carefully explained repentance, Chepe leaned against the wall and listened. Suddenly, it was just too much. He wanted to get out of there. Peering through the holes in his red mask, he snapped, "Hey, I didn't come here to be preached at. You," he demanded, pointing at Tim, "talk less and give me your watch."

Tim calmly stuck his left arm behind his back and continued, "We pray that you will be saved someday."

"Pablo, get me several flashlights," he commanded.

"*Amigo,* I only have one flashlight left. You have taken them all. And I need the last one to shine around nights."

Pablo didn't budge to get the flashlight. Suddenly, Chepe understood. The money and all the things he had in his bags were gifts. The *cheles* obviously felt that was enough for one night. They would not just hand over everything he wanted. Though there were still many salable things in that house, he had no access to them. The smiling *gringos* weren't afraid anymore.

Chepe was more than ready to leave. "*Buenas noches,*" he said quietly; then he turned and left the house faster than he had come. Once again, he heard their voices following him, "May God bless you!"

---

8 *Torch of Truth, a magazine published in Costa Rica*

As he climbed the hill behind the house, he growled to himself, *If I don't find a way to scare them, I won't be able to get things from them anymore. I have to come up with a plan.*

He arrived at the laurel tree among the grasses. First, he stripped the tight sack off his back and threw it aside. Then, taking off his mask, he wrapped it around the wooden pistol and, bending over, pushed it in among the leaves at the base of the laurel tree. *Just in case I decide to come back,* he muttered. *Next time I'll have my gear ready.*

Then Chepe trudged toward Waslala, his mind spinning. He had so much to think about. God had made a little opening into Chepe's heart, and the Holy Spirit used it to the maximum. Chepe thought about what the three *cheles* had drilled into his brain that evening. *Could I really change and become a Christian? Could I actually get to the place where I could love God so much that I'd even be willing to love my enemies? Those three cheles must think I could.*

But the devil was concerned that he was losing grip on his client. Chepe was useful in his scheming, especially in fulfilling his purposes of discouraging the missionaries. The devil attacked Chepe's mind with hundreds of thoughts that drowned out the good thoughts toward God. *You can never be a Christian. You could never be like those men. You are a permanent flop, and you will always be a robber. The next time you go see the missionaries, take some fellows along. That will scare them again, and even if you don't get much money, you can make a haul of all their things.*

The two voices continued haunting Chepe's brain during the two-hour walk to Waslala. By the time Chepe was walking up the steep Papayo Hill, there was no question which voice was winning the battle. The *gringos* would be robbed again.

Chepe used the little bit of money he got from the *gringos* to buy liquor. Carrying his bottle of *cañita*, he headed for La Poza de los Compas again. He had slept late the morning after the robbery. Now it was after ten o'clock, and he knew he would find people there. Sure enough, there were several shoe-shiners swimming in the pool and several older boys sitting among the guaba trees. Chepe headed for the guaba trees, as usual.

Cobra was there again, selling drugs to anybody who needed a puff. Among the rough-looking men lounging around under the trees, Chepe noticed Oscar, a loner like himself, puffing on a cigar. *That's my guy!* Chepe cheered inwardly. He plopped down beside his old friend and offered him drink. In exchange, Oscar gave him a cigar of the best Waslala-grown marijuana.

As the next several hours slurped and puffed by, Chepe found himself telling Oscar all about his easy robberies. "I know them," Oscar gloated. "When they first moved to Waslala, they were our neighbors. I never got close to them, but my younger brothers and sisters used to play with their children when they still lived in town. They even held a *culto* (service) for my mom at our house. I didn't go, of course. But the family knows them well. My mom thinks highly of them."

"I do too," Chepe guffawed. "They have a lot of nice things I could sell for a good price. If you and your brother would go with me, we would make a haul!"

The date was July 19, 1996. The gathering by the laurel tree was larger than usual. Chepe was there, of course, dressed in a purple, long-sleeved, checkered shirt. Oscar was a dark, skinny fellow about eighteen years old. He was dressed in poor *campesino* pants. He didn't wear a shirt. Julio was dressed in what looked like rags. He was just fourteen years old, but he was already learning the ways of his wicked brother. He was light-skinned and sickly. But he was willing to go along on any adventure whenever he had a chance.[9]

---

9 *The missionaries' side of this story can be found in* Angels Over Waslala, *chapter 38.*

"Look, boys, once we hit," Chepe explained, "you have to come over to the windows and make yourselves seen. They will be frightened when they see it's a gang. You don't have to say anything. Just stand there and look mean!"

The two boys nodded. Neither of them wanted to wear masks, but Chepe knew he couldn't afford to be seen. So he bent over and rummaged through the dead leaves at the base of the laurel tree to find his gear. It wasn't there. He knelt and frantically dug through the debris. Jumping up abruptly, he swore. Then he hissed, "Somebody stole my gun and my mask!"

"Who would have done that?" Oscar asked.

"Man, I don't know," Chepe answered. "It might have been Pablo. But how could he have known? Let's just say it was the rats. But what can I use for a mask now?"

Suddenly Chepe was jerking off his shirt. "I hate to mess up this shirt my sister Ana gave me, but I don't have another option. Here, help me Julio. Hold the shirt."

Chepe took his machete and cut off the sleeves. He stuck one sleeve in his pocket and split the other one with the sharp knife he carried in his belt. While Oscar shone with his flashlight, Chepe cut two holes for his eyes at just the right place. He slipped the sleeve over his head and tied a knot at the top. Then he plopped his bill cap over it and growled, *"Boca abajo!"*

This mask explained why the robber's shirt was sleeveless!

Oscar and Julio were laughing now. "That will really scare the *gringos!* You look a fright."

"Let's go then," Chepe announced, and the robbers' parade started down over the hill toward the *gringo's* house. It was seven o'clock, just like usual.

When the three ruffians sneaked out from behind the *rancho,* ready for the attack, the two young men were surprised how afraid they felt. They had done a lot of stealing, but never had they been involved in a holdup like this. They cowered behind Chepe, not wanting to come out into the open. "Come on out!" Chepe growled.

"What if they shoot us?"

"They won't hurt a flea!" Chepe hissed. "They don't even own guns, much less would they use them. They are Christians."

"I'm still afraid!" Oscar mumbled.

Chepe knew they needed to get going. Stepping out into the opening, he hollered in a commanding voice, *"Boca abajo."*

Almost right away, Pablo's face filled the window, looking in their direction. Chepe saw that, behind him, everybody else took off running. This time, he knew, the women and children had run upstairs. Determinedly, he marched over toward the window where Pablo waited on him. His two buddies followed in the distance. *We have to scare them,* Chepe kept reminding himself.

The dog was really angry that night, raving right between them and the open window.

"Shut that dog up!" Chepe hollered.

Pablo stepped outside with a chain and collared the dog, dragging her into the house after him. Then Chepe shouted, "Get *boca abajo!"*

Chepe was relieved to see Eldon and Pablo hit the floor again. *They saw several of us and don't know it's me this time,* he gloated. *This time I'll make my haul!*

Chepe marched right into the living room, brandishing his machete and acting tough. "Make those women come back down here," he yelled. "I saw them run. Everybody has to be here on the floor."

Pablo lifted his head from the floor and asked kindly, "Couldn't they just stay upstairs? They have been through a lot of scares . . ."

"Nope," Chepe barked. "They must come down." Then, turning to Eldon, he commanded, "You, *chele*, take me upstairs."

Oscar stood just outside the front door. He peeped around the doorjamb to see what was going on. There was Pablo all alone, lying flat. But Oscar jerked his face back when he saw Pablo peering up at him. Pablo had seen him clearly for a fraction of a second. *Will he recognize me?* Oscar wondered.

As the robber followed Eldon upstairs, he again demanded loudly, "The ladies must come downstairs and get *boca abajo*. Do you hear?"

Eldon didn't answer, but what he saw as he stepped up onto the landing gave him an idea. Turning to Chepe, he said, "Please, let them stay! Come, see what they are doing." He motioned for Chepe to step up beside him and pointed into the bedroom.

Chepe stepped up and looked into the room. He stared. What he saw pierced his tough shell and made his belligerent attitude shrink. The preacher's wife and her children were kneeling around the bed, praying. The tender scene touched the robber's heart and melted it in preparation for what was yet to come. Speechless, he turned reverently and motioned Eldon to follow him into an adjacent bedroom.

They went through Eldon's room. The room was dark, so they used Eldon's flashlight. Somehow Chepe failed to see the small fan, the tape player, the blender, and other valuables in plain sight. All Chepe took was clothing.

After Chepe ordered Eldon down on the floor again, he instructed Pablo to get up and march upstairs. He didn't say a word about the ladies in the other room, but made Pablo collect clothes from his closet. He also asked for sheets and blankets and other valuables he saw. Then, unexpectedly, Pablo stopped and whispered, "You know what, sir? I am getting an idea who you are and where you live."

"Don't you dare say that!" Chepe snarled. *The nerve!* Chepe thought. *Some robbers would kill a guy for saying that. He's trying to scare me. Apparently these people don't lie, though. That means I'm in trouble.*

The robbery took on a different dimension. Now Chepe was afraid of what Pablo knew and what he might do, and he was in a great hurry to finish.

Chepe took Pablo downstairs, where he asked for cheese and other food items. Pablo kept collecting things and handing them to Chepe. But Chepe's arms got too full, so Pablo suggested, "Let's put all this stuff on the table. Then later we can pack it all up for you."

"Get me a sack to put this stuff in," Chepe suggested.

"I'd have to go out to the *rancho* to find a sack."

"*Vamos* (let's go)," Chepe agreed.

Out in the rancho, Chepe asked for two sacks and a piece of plastic. *I will hide this stuff in the field,* he thought. *With all the rain lately, I'll need the plastic to cover the loot.*

While they were alone in the *rancho*, Chepe faced Pablo. "Who did you put on my trail?" he questioned sharply, holding his machete just right.

"What do you mean?" Pablo asked.

"Did you put the Recontra on my trail?"

"Oh, no. You know we don't do that. I haven't told the police either."

"Then why did you say you know me?" Chepe asked.

"I just found out where the *lapa* found a home. That's why I think you live in Claudia Chamorro (one of Waslala's barrios)," Pablo mentioned as they headed back to the house.

One the way back to the house, Pablo stopped suddenly, and Chepe almost rammed into him. Stepping aside, he stared at Pablo's face in the moonlight. He could see that Pablo had something important to say.

"Look," Pablo began haltingly, with a troubled look on his face. "This evening at dusk my little three-year-old daughter came to me twice and asked, 'Daddy, is the bad man coming again tonight?' "

Chepe swallowed, but kept listening.

"Don't you pity us sometimes? Tonight my wife choked her supper down while sitting on the stairway steps. Since it's been a little over two weeks, she was afraid you would come again tonight. She was too scared to eat her food downstairs, and she was afraid to eat her food upstairs all alone."

Chepe's head hung a little lower.

"My children sometimes cry when it gets dark. Put your hand here on your heart," Pablo suggested, placing his hand on his own chest. "Couldn't you have some compassion on us?"

As Pablo stood there gazing at him, Chepe could almost see tears in his eyes. What Pablo was saying was true. He realized it was time to do something about it.

"Yeah," Chepe drawled, "I know I have been nasty to you people. I do pity you sometimes. Get me two hundred córdobas, and I promise not to come back."

"I don't have two hundred córdobas. You know I don't. If I had more money, I would have given it to you."

"Get me two new Bibles then," Chepe bargained. *I can sell them easily for a day's worth of weed.*

Pablo left for the house to find the Bibles. Oscar and Julio were nowhere to be seen. Then Pablo carefully packed the loot for his friend. As Chepe watched, he could see how tenderly and willingly he packed. He filled two sacks full of goods. The last thing Pablo placed at the mouth of the sack was a big twelve-pound block of his delicious cheese. Chepe knew that selling cheese was Pablo's way of making his living. *I guess I am being hard on these people,* Chepe mused. *How many cheeses have I hauled off?*

But what really touched Chepe's heart was that, as Pablo placed the cheese into the sack, he gave it a little pat, and then, with a twinkle in his eye, he whispered, "Especially for you!"

Pablo helped Chepe carry the loot out into the yard. "Carry these sacks up to the top of the hill for me," Chepe commanded.

Pablo hesitated. Chepe could see that he didn't want to. *Maybe he doesn't want to leave his family here alone,* Chepe thought. Then he remembered that he had his buddies to help him. He was ready to turn and leave when he saw that Pablo wanted to talk again. "Listen," Pablo said, and Chepe detected a catch in his voice. "Let's make a deal. I believe you live in Claudia Chamorro. I told you that already. I believe I know which family you belong to. You stop robbing us, and I won't tell the police or turn you in to the Recontra."

Chepe's heart was moved that night. He really did pity these people. But he was also afraid. If this man told his neighbors who he thought he was, things would happen. And those things would not be good. Pablo was giving him a chance. He was ready to deal.

"If you don't tell your neighbors about tonight, I will deal," Chepe suggested.

"I can't do that. Our neighbors are the first to find out about our robberies. Tomorrow morning they will ask us if anything happened during the night, and we always tell them the truth. But I won't tell the police."

Chepe's mind raced. *He won't tell the police or the Recontra, but his neighbors will. I have to convince him not to tell the neighbors . . .*

Pablo spoke again. "This is my offer: I won't turn you in. I will give you work if you come here in the daytime. I will pray for you every day. And you will not come back again to rob us."

The offer to pray struck another chord in Chepe's heart. Not even his mama prayed for him. Not even his sister Ana, who wasn't converted. This man was willing to pray for him, his enemy, his robber. It was too much. "I want to make this deal," Chepe continued, feeling a knot in his throat, "but I want you to include that you won't tell the neighbors."

"I told you I can't do that. I can promise not to tell them who you are, since I am not sure myself, but I cannot promise that I won't tell them you came again tonight."

"Okay," Chepe answered, "it's a deal. I do feel for you and your family. I know it's hard. I don't hurt you, but it still scares you, and the children suffer. I promise that this is the last time I will steal from you."

As Chepe voiced these sincere words, he stepped closer to his friend. Pablo stepped toward him, too. What would be the most appropriate way to seal this deal? *A handshake,* Chepe concluded eagerly.

To his surprise, Pablo was not only ready to shake his hand, but wanted to do it their style. Not the formal handshake, but the way Chepe and his buddies clasped hands among them-selves—a high five ending in an upright clasp. The slap rang out into the dark night. But there was no doubt in either man's mind that the ring had also penetrated both of their hearts. It not only sealed the deal, but it was a way for both men to say, though in extremely unlikely circumstances, "I will never forget you! Not until death do us part."

Loot. Loot is always a problem. Chepe's brain was working as he and his two buddies hiked up the hill behind Pablo's place. Some years before, Oscar's brother had killed his younger brother in cold-blooded fighting over loot. *We'd just as well get it over with,* Chepe thought.

Reaching the top of the hill by the infamous laurel tree, Chepe ordered the boys to put their bags down. "Look, boys," he ordered. "I am the leader in this bunch. I did all the work. I am going to give you your share of the loot right away. That way, once we get to Waslala, everyone can go his own way."

The two boys exchanged glances in the moonlight, suddenly realizing they were not going to get much. Oscar frowned darkly. "We ran the same risk you did!" he snapped.

"Here," Chepe answered, rummaging through the bags, "I will give each of you a set of clothes and a blanket. That's plenty of loot for one night!"

"I like cheese," Julio muttered. "I'm hungry, and I saw that you have some crackers and cookies . . ."

"I want part of the money," Oscar said, his voice cold as ice.

"Money! What a joke! Those *cheles* never have any money."

"You wouldn't either if they stole from you as many times as you have stolen from them. But they did give you some. I saw him hand it to you. I want my half, and then I will share with my brother."

The two older men argued hotly. Finally, a deal was struck without any fists flying. But just as Chepe had felt several months before with Douglas, Oscar knew the truth: Chepe had ripped him off!

Efraín looked at Chepe sitting on the chair in front of him, stone drunk. "You rascal, if you know what's good for you, you'll leave Waslala. Just think about it. If you stole from any other rich guy in this town, you would already have your brains blown out. So you go on and on molesting these people who are here in this country to help the poor. You are fit to be hung!"

"I didn't hurt them," Chepe whined.

"Not physically, but psychologically. You have probably almost done them in. Didn't you just finish telling me that last week the lady ate her meal on the steps, and that cute little curly-headed *chela* was worried that you would come back? Your heart must be as hard as stone."

"I'm not . . . hic . . . going to go back. I told you."

"Let me tell you why else you won't go back. Those tapes you sold—people are talking about them all over the place. Yesterday, Pablo himself came and asked Mom if the tapes were sold from this house. You are sunk, man! Even if Pablo won't put the police on you, he's no dummy. He's determined to meet you, and when he does, everybody will find it out. Then his neighbors will take care of the rest. The people in Kusulí love and respect that guy."

"What did your mom say?" Chepe asked, his face anxious.

"She lied for you and said that you had already skipped the area. She told him that we didn't know you were a robber, but when we found out, we chased you off. He seemed satisfied and left."

"Not only that," Tirso threw in, "everybody in Claudia Chamorro knows about the *lapa* and that it used to belong to the *gringos*. Let the Recontra hear one such rumor and your throat is cut, man! If you esteem your life, run."

"I plan to leave for El Cuá tomorrow," Chepe decided on the spot. "Don't tell anybody where I am going. Would you loan me the money, Efraín?"

"I'll loan you the money," Efraín agreed. "We won't tell, but change your ways, man. And get yourself a job! Your sister Ana will help you. She always does."

Life in El Cuá didn't seem too bad at first. The town was much like Waslala. As Chepe expected, his sister took him under her wing and helped him start a job. Knowing that he was a good peddler, she bought a bunch of medicine, and he walked all over the country selling it at a small profit. Every evening they would count the money, and Chepe would give her the money for the medicine and keep the little profit for himself.

Ana tried her best to help Chepe mend his ways. Now that he had a job, he didn't need to steal. She especially encouraged him to stop drinking and doing drugs. For her sake, Chepe hid his vices and tried to prove that he was changing. But after several months, Chepe slowly slipped back into his wicked ways. Less and less often would he take his satchel and peddle his wares. More and more often he would leave home evenings and return in the wee hours of the morning.

One morning, he stumbled home drunk. Flopping down on a chair, he started to talk. His tongue always loosened when he was drunk. "You know, Ana, I miss Waslala."

"Why do you miss Waslala?" Ana asked, as she thumped away at her old treadle sewing machine.

"I had a lot of friends in Waslala," he belched. "And stealing was easy. It's too bad I didn't bring you some of the things I stole. I had a nice red tape player. I had two blenders. But I sold it all . . ."

"For drink," she finished the sentence for him. "For drink and for drugs. Why do you say stealing was easy?" Ana questioned her brother. "Stealing is never easy."

"See, I had an *amigo*," Chepe chuckled. "That's actually what he called me. He was a *gringo* and a pastor of a strange church. They believe that you aren't supposed to carry guns or hurt your enemies. They believe that you should do good to the robbers. I could never figure them out."

"How many times did you steal from them?" Ana asked, raising her eyebrows.

"Five times," Chepe answered pensively, "if I have it straight. I'd go about every two weeks to get more stuff."

"You say he was a good man and was nice to you," Ana said sharply. "Then why did you steal from him again and again?"

"I don't know," Chepe sighed. "I guess I just missed him and had to go back." Chepe burst out laughing at his own joke.

"They were probably missing you, too," Ana retorted darkly. "Man, you were mean!"

"I know I was," Chepe acknowledged. "That's why I finally stopped stealing from them."

"I still want to know why you did it," Ana insisted.

"I guess it was because it was so easy. If I steal here in El Cuá, I have to be so careful. I have to be ready to run because I might get shot. At the *gringo's* place, I would just walk up to their window and holler '*Boca abajo!*' and they would hit the floor and lie there with their little rumps in the air. I could just help myself." Chepe was laughing again. "Even the little children hit the floor. They all had so much practice. The lady would sing to her little girl from the floor . . ."

Ana was getting angry. "You should be ashamed of yourself, Chepe Rodriguez! I can't imagine the fear those poor people suffered."

"I'll never forget the time I took their *lapa*," Chepe said, suddenly turning serious. "I was wearing a black plastic hood and a black plastic mask. The *gringo* had just given me all that I had asked for, even their favorite pet. Then that man put his hand on my shoulder and told me that he loved me. That was the first time in my life someone told me they loved me."

Tears were streaming down the drunken man's face now. "It's also the first time a man I robbed told me he loved me."

"Probably the last time, too!" Ana reminded him. "Go and see if you can find somebody in El Cuá who will say that when they find you stealing! They'll say 'I love you' with a bullet! Chepe, I am worried for you. Your heart is as hard as a rock!"

Chepe dried his tears, and then he smiled. "Ana, you should have been there the time I assaulted them with a hand grenade."

"Where did you get a hand grenade?" Ana asked, mortified.

"In the cacao patch," Chepe roared, slapping his hand on his leg. "It was a cacao fruit that was half rotten. I tell you, it looked real. Another time I used a pistol that I carved out of wood. Oh, did I scare those poor people that time!"

"Chepe, I am ashamed of you," Ana answered angrily, pointing her finger at him. "You are too wicked for me. I have a feeling you are stealing here in El Cuá, too! If you are, I won't lift a finger to help you when you get in trouble."

"No, no," Chepe pleaded. "I don't steal here. I . . . I wouldn't do that."

"Where did you get the money to buy the bicycle you ride these days?"

"A guy gave it to me. Ana, I really have to go. I promised a guy to help him work today," Chepe finished the conversation abruptly, jumping up from his chair. He stumbled as he left the room. Ana watched him go, shaking her head. *Chepe is a dead duck. If he keeps on like that someone will kill him. How I pity those poor gringos from Waslala!*

Chepe walked up to Billetón's place carrying a large, fancy stereo on his shoulder, listening to a song called *La Puerta*

Negra (The Black Door). Grinning like an opossum, he saluted everybody and plopped down on the chair on the porch. Billetón stood there and stared at him.

Billetón was Efraín and Tirso's father. He had left their mother and moved to El Cuá a few years before. Chepe knew Billetón hated his stealing but tolerated him as a person. Billetón was a man of means and owned two bus lines in El Cuá. He had often tried to help Chepe, but had given up on him long ago.

"Where did you get that stereo?" Billetón asked cautiously.

"Oh, a friend loaned it to me. I love music. Do you want to hear a tape? It's in English." Chepe turned the tape player on and the Living Stones Quartet sang. "Thank you, Jesus, for salvation full and free . . ."

"I know where you got that cassette!" Billetón snapped. "You *sinvergüenza* (shameless one) stole it from the *gringos* in Kusulí. I wonder where you stole that fancy stereo."

Just then one of Billetón's oldest sons rushed on the scene. "Hey, Chepe," the young man gasped, "I ran all the way from Ana's house to warn you. The police are searching her house right now. They are looking for you. There was a robbery last night at a farm across the river. They claim it was you. If I were you, I'd run!"

Chepe plopped the recorder on the porch, forgetting it completely. "Loan me a hundred córdobas," he urged, turning to Billetón. "I've got to go. I'm moving to Paiwas, out close to Río Blanco. Pedro Hondureño is constantly inviting me to come over to live with him."

Billetón handed Chepe a hundred córdoba bill. Chepe seemed calm as he jumped on the bus at the corner. Billetón hid the stereo.

All day long, Ana and Billetón and the rest of the family waited to hear the news. They were sure Chepe would be in jail before the day was over. They heard that the police had stopped the bus several kilometers out of town. But Chepe had not been on it. He had disappeared into thin air.

Later, a friend of Chepe's who was on the same bus stopped at Billetón's place to give him the news. "That stinker Chepe has a sixth sense. He was sitting on the bus as if nothing was wrong. Suddenly he decided to get off. Just around the next corner were the police, waiting for him. He got away as clean as a morning after the rain!"

"That's Chepe for you," Billetón answered. "He never seems to get caught. But someday his stealing will catch up with him."

The bus ground to a stop on the dusty, rut-riven street. Ana stepped off, tired and grimy. "Where will I stay in this godforsaken place?" she muttered to herself. "I don't know anyone here."

Ana knew Chepe had moved to the little town of Paiwas after fleeing from El Cuá in 1997. She also knew he had shacked up with a woman there and had a little boy. She had an address for the place where they supposedly lived. It was 2003, six years after Chepe had moved away. The first two years they had heard from him in roundabout ways. But they hadn't heard a thing from him or about him in four years.

Ana walked the narrow streets of Paiwas, fearing the worst. She found the simple wooden house late in the afternoon. A little five-year-old boy was playing on the porch. An old man sat on a rickety chair close to the child, as if watching out for him. The little boy stopped and stared at Ana as she walked up to the porch. Then, jumping up and down like a kangaroo, he fled.

Ana stared as the child disappeared into the house. It had to be Chepe's little boy. He had Chepe's big brown eyes and wild spirit. Soon a young lady in tattered clothes walked out to meet Ana, the little banshee hanging onto her skirt.

After exchanging greetings, Ana got right to the point. "I am Chepe Rodríguez's sister. I came to visit him. Is he around?"

The lady's face turned pale. Fidgeting, she looked over at the man who was obviously her father. "Chepe got killed four years ago already," he said coldly.

Ana was shocked. But in her heart she had known that four years of silence could mean only one thing. Chepe was gone.

"What happened?" she stammered.

"They caught him down by the river one night. They hacked him into pieces with machetes."

"Why didn't you let us know?" Ana asked, her chest heaving. She felt like screaming, but she knew she must control her emotions. She was a stranger, in a strange place, among strange people.

"We tried to let you know," the lady answered. "We announced it on the radio."

"The radio stations from here never reach El Cuá!" Ana retorted. "Why didn't you send someone on the bus to tell us?"

"We were broke," the lady answered lamely.

The gruff old man looked up. "We did what we could. If you didn't find out, it's not our fault."

"Why did they kill him?" Ana asked next. "I'd like to hear the story."

"We never really knew what happened," the woman lied. "He evidently had an enemy. One night this enemy stopped him down by the river, drunk. Chepe never had a chance. We gathered the pieces and buried them in the local graveyard. Would you like to go see the burial spot?"

"No," Ana replied sadly. "It won't bring my brother back to life. By the way, what's your name?"

"My name is Vilma Molinares. We called our little boy Chepe after his daddy. Do you think he looks like him?"

"He sure does," Ana agreed. "He acts like Chepe did when he was little. Wild and rambunctious, just like that little kid. And he has the same big, brown eyes."

Ana stayed the night with Vilma, who told her stories about their life in Paiwas, carefully avoiding mention of Chepe's stealing. Ana had to read between the lines. As the evening progressed, she learned the truth. Chepe had never stopped stealing until the day he died.

The next day, Ana decided to find out how her brother had died. Surely someone would tell her the truth. She chose to visit the store nearest Vilma's house. When old Tilo heard that Ana was Chepe's sister, he invited her into his living room and told her the sad story of her brother's death.

Tilo was frank. "Vilma will never tell you the truth," he assured her.

Ana nodded. "I already figured that out."

"Chepe and Pedro Hondureño were unhandy robbers in this town. They broke into my store once and made a haul. I found out who had done it, but chose to let it go. I did not want those two for my enemies."

"Did he get killed for stealing?" Ana asked.

Tilo shook his head sadly. "No. He would've eventually gotten killed for stealing, but he got killed because of Vilma."

"Vilma?" Ana asked, astonished.

"After Chepe shacked up with Vilma, they lived together in a poor shack. That's where little Chepito was born. After he was about a year old, Patricio, a friend of Chepe's, invited Chepe and Vilma to move in with him. See, Chepe was so poor that they didn't have any furniture and barely had even dishes or kettles to cook with. Their lives were pathetic. Patricio had a house of his own and was set up better. Patricio and his woman couldn't have children. So when they invited Chepe and Vilma to move in with them, they did."

"Did Patricio steal with him?"

"Not that I know of. Actually, he worked for Patricio for a while and tried to reform. But several things led to trouble. First, Patricio was having serious problems with his wife. Soon after Chepe and Vilma moved in, she left him. Second, Patricio had a terrible temper.

"The new arrangement was really good for Patricio. Since his woman had left him, Vilma cooked for them both. Soon Patricio took a liking to little Chepito. And then he took a liking to Vilma, too. That's when the trouble started. Chepe soon suspected the truth, and his relationship with Patricio deteriorated fast."

Ana nodded, urging him on.

"Eventually Patricio came up with a plan to get rid of Chepe. One evening in November of 1999, Patricio took Chepe out to the town's tavern. He got Chepe so drunk he barely knew what was going on. Then Patricio went home and locked himself into his house with Vilma. 'When your man comes back, we will just tell him that it's over. He'll go back to El Cuá or Waslala, and I will keep you,' Patricio promised. Thinking of all the financial benefits, and tired of living with a robber, Vilma agreed.

"Chepe came back and tried to get into the house. From inside, Patricio told Chepe how things stood. He told him that Vilma agreed and that he should get out of there before he got mad. He figured Chepe would give up easily and leave. But he didn't.

"Chepe got very angry. He cursed and swore and tried to break in the door. This made Patricio furious.

" 'Get out of here, you rascal!' Patricio yelled. 'This is my private property, and I will take you to the law if you don't stop!'

"Suddenly, Chepe thought of a way to pressure his enemy. Patricio's dad was Chepe's friend. He was also a man of a great temper and knew good and well that Vilma was Chepe's woman. So Chepe hollered, 'Give me my woman back or I am going to tell your dad what you are doing. I am going right now.'

"Chepe stumbled off to find Patricio's father. That was the last straw for Patricio. Blinded by rage, he followed Chepe. Taking another trail, he waited by the river just before his father's place. Just as Chepe stepped out of the water, Patricio jumped out and butchered him with his machete. Chepe had no weapon to defend himself with, and he was too drunk anyway. Patricio had only drunk enough to be wild and crazy."

Ana was shaking and tears welled in her eyes.

"Do you want me to describe what he looked like?" Tilo asked.

"No," Ana pleaded, raising both of her hands. "That's enough. Vilma already told me that when they went to get him to bury him, they brought him in pieces."

"That's right," Tilo said. "Even the policemen were shocked. Patricio skipped the country. Nobody knows where he went. Vilma and little Chepito moved back to her parents' place."

It was raining as Ana rode the bus toward Matagalpa. Raindrops ran down the steamed-up bus windows. Teardrops ran down Ana's cheeks as she reviewed Chepe's life story. His was indeed a story of a life gone awry.

Chepe left this world as a man without hope. His final destination was not what he wanted, but it was the consequence of his choices. Hell. God, in love, had extended His hand of mercy time and again to give this poor man a chance. Chepe could have sought counsel and help from God and the brethren instead of stealing from them. But Chepe rejected God's special agents and His golden opportunities. And he paid the price of rejection.

Chapter Two
SKINNED ALIVE

The night seemed dark under the canopy of trees. So dark that only a kinkajou (nocturnal, monkey-like animal) would have been able to see the man and the boy wading through the creek, water sloshing in their rubber boots. The two were dressed in poor *campesino* clothes, their bill caps cocked backwards. Beto, the leader, held a long, sharp machete. Franklin, his helper, carried a knife in his belt and a sack under his arm.

"Quiet," Beto hissed. "We don't want that dog barking when we load the chickens. We need silence."

Franklin nodded, but Beto couldn't see him. Leaving the creek, they began to climb a steep trail up a twenty-foot bank through a thick stand of jungle and bamboo. Franklin slipped and fell. Beto scolded his nephew and hissed at him.

They came to the edge of the jungle and stepped out into the clearing. Franklin stayed behind Beto. Though it wasn't Franklin's first time on a mission like this, he was still a little nervous. He was only thirteen. Beto was twenty-five and an experienced robber.

The moon was shining brightly. Holding completely still, the two stared at the distant barn looming up out of the grasses. Beyond the barn stood the two-story wooden house. "I hope they're sleeping soundly, as usual," Beto whispered. Then he chuckled. "Remember when we came and got their pet deer? They never heard a thing, and the dog never barked once."

Franklin was laughing quietly. "Yeah, that was the easiest meat we got in a long time. What a party we had that night! And tonight it will be chicken. Yum! I'm starving!"

"Okay, the chickens are here on this end of the barn, right?" Beto asked.

From previous experience in hanging around the neighborhood, Franklin knew Pablo's place well. "Yes, there's a lean-to on this end of the barn. That's where they roost. They have free run of the fenced area where the deer used to roam. We have to sneak up and open the door into the lean-to. Then it's simple—we grab the chickens and run."

Halfway across the grassy field was a bushy tree boxed in by a barbed-wire fence. The grass had grown tall within the little enclosure, making an excellent hideout in the otherwise weedless field.

"Let's stand behind this clump for a while to make sure they are asleep," Beto suggested. As they watched and waited, peeping out from behind the tree, Beto told Franklin what else he had on his mind. "The next time we get meat, we're going to be really bold. You told me they have a *guardiola* (paca) in a cage behind the house."

"They sure do! The thing is roly-poly fat and would make great eating! But we could never get it, because the dog would bark and they would find us out."

"No, sirree. We'll come when they are in church some Wednesday evening. By the time they get back, we'll be cooking up a storm!"

"You're right, Uncle. Let's do it!"

Beto glanced at his nephew. Franklin was short for his age and dark-skinned. He always had been a wiry young fellow who loved excitement and hated work. So Beto taught him how to make money without working, and Franklin joined his band of robbers. Never having enjoyed a close relationship with his parents, Franklin was a loner, and he had always liked mischief. As he got older, he loved to get into trouble. Everybody said he was turning out badly, and he seemed determined to prove them right.

It wasn't long before Beto realized his little pipsqueak of a nephew was even more rebellious than he was, and he had more nerve, too. Yet Beto never warned Franklin about the dangers and difficulties of his trade. Probably Franklin would not have listened anyway.

The two men slipped into the shadow of the barn. They made their way over to the lean-to and silently let themselves into the chicken pen. Beto whispered, "You get a chicken and I get a chicken. Grab it by its neck and choke it right away. Then we leave as quietly as we can. If they squawk, we run and hide behind that tree again. Ready?"

Under the low eaves of the lean-to, the chickens stretched out their necks in apprehension, hearing the whispers and seeing the shadows moving in the moonlight. The big black hen Franklin chose was a little too high for him to reach. In his eagerness, he grabbed the hen by her wing. She squawked vehemently, desperately trying to break away from his grasp. Franklin released the hen and ran. Beto had not grabbed his hen yet, but he was already running. The dog barked furiously as she charged toward the barn. Beto and Franklin raced behind the bushy tree and flung themselves onto the grass, laughing.

As soon as they could control their laughter, they peeped out through the tall grass. "Pablo turned a light on," Franklin hissed.

"That's right," Beto answered. "But he won't come out here. They have had so many robbers hold them up with guns that they are too scared to go out nights."

"So we're safe here?" Franklin asked.

"Absolutely! Let's just wait until his light goes off. Then we'll go get those chickens! And this time you choke them right, you skunk!"

The two men relaxed, expecting to wait half an hour. Suddenly a light shone out into the field toward them. The two men buried themselves deeper into the grass and held perfectly still.

"He came out, after all," Franklin hissed.

"But he won't think of coming down here," Beto insisted. "If we hold still, we'll be safe. Besides, even if he would find us, that preacher wouldn't hurt a flea."

"That's right," Franklin giggled. "But I'd still hate to get caught. If he comes down this way, I'm running down into that jungle as fast as I can!"

"Me, too!" Beto assured him.

Watching intently, they could see Pablo's silhouette as he shone the light around in the lean-to. After what seemed like a long time, he stepped out into the moonlit field. The bandits could see him as plain as day. They got onto their knees, ready to run. "I bet he's as angry as a hornet." Beto grinned nervously.

"I bet the devil is choking him," Franklin mocked.

Suddenly the silence of the night was broken by a loud shout that echoed across the grasses and bounced off the jungle wall. Four words, clearly spoken. Unmistakable words, which shocked the two robbers to the core. "*¡Que Dios les bendiga!* (May God bless you!)"

As the robbers stared, the preacher turned, and they could see the light bobbing as he headed back to his house, his head bowed. Beto almost pitied the man. They had been robbed so many times, and now his chickens were disappearing, too. "Let's go, Franklin," Beto said soberly.

"What do you mean, let's go?" Franklin retorted. "Not take any chickens home? Never! Even Grandma is looking forward to the chicken soup we'll have cooking by morning."

So Beto was persuaded to go back again, even if he was still blushing from the blessing they had received. Later, as they waded up the stream again, loaded with six of the missionary's chickens, Beto knew he was being mean. But Franklin cheered and laughed. This was the life he loved. It would take more than the blessings of a preacher to stop him from stealing.

Harold lived in a place called Dipina, fifteen miles in the outback, northeast from Waslala. He was angry, very angry. Two young neighbors, sons of a man named Santiago, were constantly causing trouble. Lately, the dispute was where the line fence was supposed to run between their two properties. Harold had decided to put the fence where he thought it should be, but the brothers had opposed and forced him to remove it.

A feud had raged between these two farming families for years. In addition to the two boys who made Harold move his fence, Santiago had several other sons. Harold had three sons. The blood on both sides was running hot.

Harold called his sons together. "Look, boys," Harold began, "this has gone too far. If we don't put a stop to this, it will bring us to ruin. We are going to have to kill some of them so they leave us in peace. We can't do the dirty work, because they would catch on easily. We have to pay someone to do it for us and have witnesses that we were at home behaving ourselves. I would like to get rid of the two boys who are being so vocal about the fence deal. Who could we get to do the job?"

One of Harold's sons grinned. "I know a young druggie so ruthless he would gladly do this for some cash. He's from Waslala, but has relatives just over the hill. We've done some drinking together, and he tells me all kinds of stories when he's drunk. He loves to steal. His name is Franklin. He'll be our hit man."

Eventually, Harold and Franklin agreed on a price. Franklin talked to his friend, Rigo, also from Waslala, and asked him to help. Their hatred and anger grew as the plan developed.

Finally, the day came. Harold's family went to a public place, all except one of the boys. He went with Franklin and Rigo so they would be sure to get the right men. Franklin carried Harold's semi-automatic rifle. They knew the two sons would ride in from town that afternoon. The three boys waited in a clump of trees at a lonely place beside the trail.

As the time approached, Franklin's hands were trembling. He was only fifteen years old. It was going to be harder to kill than he had expected. His mouth went dry. Shaking his head to clear his mind, he steeled his heart. *I will do this. I have always dreamed of killing someone. Today I will kill two. I will not be afraid. I am tough, and today I will be really malo (bad). This is my day to prove it.*

Two horses became visible on the muddy trail. As they drew closer, Harold's son hissed, "These are our men!"

The three men closed in, still hidden by the brush. Suddenly, they leapt out onto the trail in front of the horses, while Harold's son cursed and swore at his enemies. The horses reared and wheeled around. Franklin fired immediately. He didn't want to give the men a chance to draw their own pistols. The two men fell off their fleeing horses. Franklin continued pumping them full of bullets until his gun was empty and the two men were dead.

The three killers ran. Harold's son raced to join his family, so no one would suspect him. Franklin and Rigo returned to Waslala, taking advantage of the darkness which soon swallowed their awful deed. The neighbors found the bodies at dusk. By then, Franklin and his crony were miles away.

Franklin never dreamed it would be so terrible to kill a man, or that remorse and guilt would plague him so. Fear gripped him, and his nights were filled with horrible nightmares. During the day, he drowned his misery with marijuana and liquor. Nights, he suffered and fought with his feelings and fears.

Franklin hardened his heart to the awful feelings that hounded him. He bragged and told his friends what all he had done. He forced himself to believe that he really was as tough and wicked as he claimed. But fear was still winning the fierce battle, and the poor young man was soon at his wits' end.

What Franklin didn't realize was that the heavenly Father loved him and was trying to stop him in his tracks. God wanted him to turn from his wicked ways and repent. Though Franklin didn't understand what was happening, God was ready to give him some good opportunities to seek Him and to find Him. And that would bring some big surprises into this wicked young man's life.

"I'll meet you in Kusulí by the clinic gate Wednesday evening at dusk," Franklin told his three buddies. "We'll start the operation as soon as it's good and dark. Tim and his family will be in church. That will make our job easier."

The robbers nodded eagerly. They had met Franklin in Waslala for a couple rounds of marijuana. The three brothers sold the stuff, and Franklin was one of their steady customers.

"Don't be late! We'll get them good. See you on Wednesday," Franklin laughed, puffing away on his high-powered, homemade cigar.

When the three brothers were on their way to the clinic the next Wednesday, they met a jeep with a trailer full of people heading for Waslala. A *gringo* riding on the back of the trailer smiled and waved at them.

"There they go," one of the brothers gloated. "We're free to do our job now!"

They met Franklin at the clinic gate and hid in the clinic's coffee patch until dark. Then they crossed the fields and approached Tim's house from the hidden side under the cover of darkness. They first tried to open the doors and windows, but all were securely locked. Franklin brought out the bar he carried for that purpose. In a matter of minutes, he had torn two boards off the door. Then he crawled in and opened the latch from the inside. "The house is ours!" he hissed. "Everybody to your jobs."

Soon they were boldly flipping on lights and helping themselves to whatever they could find. They emptied knapsacks to fill them with loot. One boy found a sewing machine and plopped it in a box. Another one stole dishes. Franklin found a big, box-type recorder and prepared it for travel. He also dumped a whole stack of cassettes into the box to take along home with them.

After a half hour of looting and tearing up the house, the lights suddenly went out. Since the generator was not running, the inverter was using juice from a battery pack. Now the batteries were dead, and so were the lights. This frightened the four boys, and they ran. But they soon saw no one was around, so they returned to ransack the house using a flashlight they found. They pulled out drawers and strewed the clothes all over the floor. They jerked out storage boxes and dumped the contents. They even took time to eat some of the food.

Time ticked away faster than they realized. It was almost eight o'clock when they heard the roar of the generator, which was housed in a small cement building across the creek. As the generator roared to life, the lights came back on. Franklin knew what was happening. Tim and his family were home. Tim had parked his jeep beside the generator house, started the generator, and the family would soon walk across the footbridge and up the hill. "Grab your stuff and run!" he shouted. "They'll be here in less than five minutes!"

Frantically, the boys grabbed their loot and raced behind the barn like a bunch of pack rats. Then they slid on down over the hill toward the overgrown creek bed.

Franklin was laughing. To him, this was the best kind of sport. He loved the feeling in his chest when his blood pumped with extra adrenalin. The adventure and the daring of it all fed his distorted, perverted ego. He didn't once stop to think how vulnerable Tim's family would feel as they approached their house to find the doors open and the lights on, their belongings ransacked and looted. Not only were many of their precious things missing, but what they had left was crumpled, dirty, or broken.

Franklin didn't know that Tim had already been talking to God about his material belongings. He didn't know that Tim had actually prayed that, if he was too materialistic, God would allow something to be taken away from him. Franklin didn't realize that when Tim strode through the house that night and saw the damage, he first struggled with anger. Then, remembering his sincere prayer to God, he stepped outside to get hold of his emotions. Feeling reproached for his anger, he looked up into the skies and said, "Thank you, God!" And he meant it. Peace returned to his heart.

Franklin and his cronies were loaded down as they walked toward Waslala, laughing, smoking marijuana, and bragging about what they would do with the money from the loot. Franklin didn't know what Tim and his precious family were going through at the very same time. He didn't know, and he didn't care.

But God cared. He consoled Tim and his family. He also saw Franklin's heartless attitude and frowned deeply.

Franklin thought stealing from the Christians was easy. This was true—for the moment. Tim didn't try to find out who stole his things. He didn't go hound the police so they would track them down. But he did a lot of praying.

Franklin didn't know that. Had he known the truth—that, in the long run, it was much simpler to steal from worldlings who got angry, pulled guns, and called the police—he might have chosen to be someplace else that Wednesday night. Franklin did not realize that he was playing a dangerous game when he interfered with God's children—at least not yet.

Several months later, Pablo was called to the police station. Rodolfo, chief of the Waslala police, handed him a cassette inscribed, "The Pablo Yoder Family."

"Is this yours?" he asked.

"Our family made this tape, yes," Pablo said. "But I think this is Tim Schrock's copy."

"Did Tim lose it?"

"Yes, they had a robbery several months ago. The robbers took their tape player and a whole stack of tapes. This was probably one of them."

"That's what we thought." Rodolfo grinned. "Tell Tim to come in here tomorrow. We found a cache of stolen goods in a house here in Waslala. We think a lot of the things are theirs. This tape proves that the three boys who live in that house were involved in their robbery."

When Tim and his wife, Rosa, came to the police station to identify their things, they were surprised to see Franklin's grandparents there, too. The police had also searched their house, where Franklin was staying, and had confiscated a sewing machine and some dishes that did not look like Wasla-la dishes, including a fancy glass bowl which the police felt sure was Tim's. Franklin's grandmother was crying when Tim strode in. "That precious bowl was a gift from my mother-in-law!" she wept.

Rodolfo asked Tim, "Is this your bowl?"

Tim looked at the bowl thoughtfully. "Well, my wife had a bowl like that, but this lady can have it."

"No," Rodolfo countered. "That's not right. If we just let her have the stolen stuff, the stealing will never stop. We think they are covering up for their grandson."

"I can call my wife in and ask her. She's right out here in the jeep," Tim replied.

"Go get her."

Rosa stared at her precious bowl. "Yes, it looks like mine. It's been missing since the robbery. But please, let the lady have it."

"It's mine!" the grandma insisted. "My mother-in-law—"

"Shut up!" Rodolfo snapped. Then, turning to Rosa, he asked her kindly, "Lady, did your bowl have any defects?"

"Yes," Rosa answered slowly. "It had a little chip on the edge."

Rodolfo handed the bowl to Rosa triumphantly. "You know what's yours. This bowl has a little chip on the edge." He turned to a deputy. "Get the sewing machine and all those dishes. This stuff is all theirs."

Then, turning to the grandparents, he rebuked them. "You ruin your children! You don't steal yourselves, but you are accomplices. You are happy for all the things your robbers bring home. Then you lie and make up stories to protect them. You are a bunch of *sinvergüenzas* (without shame)! I should stick you in jail, too. Go home and learn your lesson!"

The church house was packed. The music was so loud Franklin could feel vibrations through his whole body, and especially in his brain. The beat shook his body as they sang the little song again, clapping as loudly as they could. The people around him were jumping already. He wasn't sure if he wanted to jump or not. Maybe he should do like the rest. But he waited and sang on.

Ya llegó, ya llegó, ¡el Espíritu Santo ya llegó!
Ya llegó, ya llegó, ¡el Espíritu Santo ya llegó!
(He came, He came, the Holy Spirit already came!)

It had been twenty minutes now, and they were still clapping, singing a sequence of short songs over and over again. The musicians dripped with sweat. The watching crowd dripped with sweat. But in the front of the church house, beyond the rope dividing the front from the back, the ones who came to the *encuentro* (encounter) to find Jesus were drenched. Some had been jumping with the music for twenty minutes. Others, like Franklin, had just started ten minutes ago. The men jumped on one side, the women on the other.

Among the frenzied crowd were some men and women who weren't jumping. They were called *sirvientes* (servers). They had to be alert and ready. After twenty minutes, people started to fall onto the hard cement floor. The *sirvientes* caught them on the way down and tried to lay them gently among the jumping feet. As the people fell faster and faster, the servants had to be careful so that one wouldn't fall on another. That was a big job.

Franklin was one of the last to fall. The top half of his body felt as if it were empty. He felt like weeping, as wave after wave of emotion surged through his body. *Is this the Holy Spirit washing over me?* Franklin wondered as he crumpled. A *sirviente* caught him and laid him among the prostrate bodies.

Many were still twitching and groveling on the cement floor, wet with sweat and tears. After Franklin fell, his body lurched around on the floor for another ten minutes until the music stopped. After it was over, they carried him out of the church house like a dead man and laid him on the porch, where he would lay until he came to.

The *encuentro* lasted three days. During the morning hours, various religious teachers taught the attendees about the Bible. In the evenings, they held emotionally-charged services where they sang and jumped and were slain in the Spirit. Franklin, the robber, was one of that crowd. However, he wasn't sure just what was happening to him.

The last evening Franklin was awakening from his stupor. He remembered how his family members had begged him to go to the *encuentro* so he would change his life. They even paid his fee to get in. He'd had all kinds of mixed feelings as he heard the ministers teach how a person should live. And he couldn't understand the emotional experience he'd had every evening when he fell. Was he being born again, or was this just some emotional upheaval?

Franklin knew that hundreds of people were coming to a special service to receive the converts that evening. He knew that many of his evangelical relatives would be there, eager to see a changed man. Franklin also knew that they asked for testimonies at the end of the special service. He wondered if he would be brave enough to go up to the microphone.

Fully awake now, Franklin joined those who had been slain in the Spirit at the front of the church house. People started pouring in. Among them he saw his dad, his grandfather, and some of his uncles and aunts. All kinds of emotions filled his heart again. Could he prove to them that he was changed?

After a short service, the leaders invited people up front to testify. After several people wept into the mic, telling how they had been saved, Franklin stumbled up, too. He still felt weak all over, emotionally spent after three high-powered days. He clutched the mic and thought about his family watching him speak behind a pulpit for the first time. He started to cry. "I've been such a wicked sinner," he choked. He didn't know what all he was going to say in his confession. The leaders emphasized that you shouldn't plan a speech—just say on. So he did.

"I have drunk whisky, smoked marijuana, and done many other bad things." Franklin noticed how the people listened to him. It felt as if he had some strange power while standing up there. His dad's eyes were glued on him. Shaking like a leaf in the wind, he hollered into the mic, "I have stolen. I even killed some guys . . ."

Way in the back of the building, two men jerked up their heads. They whispered to each other. Franklin finished his confession, and the crowd clapped. But the two men in the back didn't. They slipped out into the darkness and disappeared.

––––––––––

The police caught Franklin at home at 4:30 a.m. They simply surrounded the house and barked orders to open up. Franklin's father and grandfather knew what the police wanted. They knew they weren't in trouble, but that Franklin surely was. So they opened up, and soon Franklin was walking toward town, handcuffed and followed by three policemen.

As they walked along, Franklin was thinking. *How did they find out I shot those two men? Something went wrong. I might be in jail for a long, long time!*

The Waslala jail was no fun. His cement cell was small and well-barred. A cement platform served as his bed. Behind the short cement partition was the shower. In the same room was a bucket which, Franklin suddenly realized, would serve as his commode. The paint in the cells was old and peeling. Graffiti covered the walls. The worst thing about the whole filthy place was that it stank so badly. The prisoners usually had to wash down their own cells daily, but there had been no water at the police station for three days. Franklin felt almost dizzy sitting there on his hard bed and smelling the stench.

The first day no one brought him food. He went to bed hungry that night and had no blanket. By midnight, he was trembling with cold. He finally dozed fitfully. He had plenty of time to think. Hours to think how it felt to be the big, tough, wicked guy . . . now behind bars. Suddenly, it was not funny after all.

His family brought him food the next day. He devoured it like a hungry bear. He also had his first interrogation session. A tall, dark-skinned man, Rodolfo Amador, knew how to get the truth out of his jailbirds. But after an hour of asking questions, Rodolfo shook his head. *It looks like he's innocent after all. The story told by the family of the two dead brothers doesn't sound nearly as believable as this boy's. I will turn him loose tomorrow,* Waslala's top policeman concluded. *There's just no proof!*

Franklin sat in his cell, grinning. *I made him believe me,* he gloated. *Never will I let them catch me again!*

That afternoon, Franklin's stomach was growling again. He'd had only one decent meal in two days. He sat on his cement bed, wondering about his future. Did they have proof that he had killed the two men? Would they condemn him to spend the rest of his life in prison? His thoughts were many and troubled. Suddenly, one of the guards approached his cell and, opening the lock, barked, "There's a man here to see you. He says he's a preacher. Follow me."

The guard led Franklin to a large barred room where they sometimes let the prisoners visit with a friend. As Franklin entered the room, he was surprised to see Pablo, the pudgy *gringo* preacher. He was standing at the far end of the room, smiling.

The guard left the room and locked the door behind them. Pablo stepped over to Franklin and shook his hand. "How are you doing, Franklin?"

"Just fine," Franklin answered, forcing a smile.

"Are you sure?" the preacher asked gently.

"Well, as fine as a guy can be behind bars. But do you know what, Pablo? I'm innocent of what they accuse me of."

"I didn't come to see if you are innocent or not. That's the judge's job. I got a call on the radio this morning from Tim."

Franklin sensed Pablo's eyes watching him closely.

"Tim told me you were in jail. I didn't even know it. He has a commitment today and couldn't come see you. He says they are planning to turn you loose tomorrow, so he wanted me to come see you today. Of course, I was glad to."

Franklin's heart did a little flip-flop when he heard they might release him the next day. That was better than he had dared expect. He grinned. "What would Tim have wanted with me?"

"I am sure he wanted to witness to you, and tell you that he forgives you."

"Forgives me for what?"

"Aw, you know. Do you know what, Franklin? Whether you are guilty of killing those two men or not, God is giving you a golden opportunity to stop and think on your ways. This is a time to reflect on the road you have chosen . . ."

Franklin listened well. He nodded pensively.

"Do you know that God loves you?"

"Yeah, I went to the *encuentro* the other day, and I'm sure God loves me. He loves me so much, Pablo. You should see what all He's done for me. I used to drink and smoke, and now I do none of those things . . ."

"Great! I'm glad you accepted Christ. But look, you have to start by being honest. Honest with yourself, with God, and

with man. That's where you start. Confess the fact that you
have stolen—"

"Who says I've stolen?" Franklin asked, his face as blank as
a cloudless sky.

"Now, come on! That's what I'm saying. You will never get
anywhere denying facts. We all know you steal. But God loves
you anyway. You are young, Franklin. You can still go straight.
It's your decision. I would be glad to help you."

Franklin hung his head.

"Look, if I were you, I would start praying. Kneel on that hard
cement bed in the cell and pray. Pray until you get through to
God. Then after that, go make your things right."

The missionary hesitated a bit, then plunged on. "Do you
know what you should do? As soon as you get out of here, go
tell Tim and Rosa you are sorry. Go back to all the people you
stole from and make all your things right."

Franklin nodded, tears in his eyes.

"May I pray for you?" Pablo suggested.

Franklin nodded again.

Pablo laid his hand on Franklin's shoulder and prayed his
heart out for the young man who seemed touched by the Gospel. Among all the things he asked of God, one struck Franklin
again. "And Lord, please give this young man the courage to
make his things right. Help him to be bold enough to say he's
sorry to Tim and to anyone else he stole from. Help him be
free."

When Pablo was ready to leave, Franklin told him he was
hungry. So Pablo promised to go buy him some food. Minutes
later, a plate of chicken from a nearby restaurant and a bottle
of Coca-Cola were brought in to the hungry man. It was one of
the tastiest meals he had ever eaten.

Back in his cell, Franklin had much to think about. *Never has
anyone treated me like that. Think of it, these are the very people I*

rob. It seems the more you steal from them, the more they love you. Tim himself wanted to come see me! I can't believe that! What he says is probably true, but there is no way I can ever be a Christian like that. I could never stop being bad. But maybe I will do what he says . . .

The next day, Franklin was released for lack of evidence. He snickered as he left the police station.

For the next several weeks, Franklin tried hard to go straight. He remembered Pablo's advice and went to Tim's house. Calling Tim aside, he asked forgiveness for breaking into his house and stealing. Tim forgave him easily and advised him to follow the Lord and to obey His Word. At the end of the conversation, Franklin asked Tim if he would loan him some money. That made Tim wonder if he was really sorry for his sins or if he just knew Tim would have a soft heart after the confession.

Franklin also asked his uncle for forgiveness for having stolen things from him. His uncle forgave him. The family and the neighborhood watched to see if Franklin's change was genuine, and, most of all, whether it would last.

Franklin needed money. He was smoking marijuana again and had no money to buy any. His addiction was driving him crazy. So his crazed mind started scheming again. In desperation, he met with his cronies in Waslala and a new plan developed.

It was 11 p.m. when they sneaked up the hill to where Carl Gingerich, the *gringo's* clinic director, lived. Franklin and his three buddies gathered for a conference in the coffee patch on the hill behind the house. They spent an hour smoking pot and making their plans.

"Carl is off to the U.S.," Franklin explained. "We'll break in that back porch and just help ourselves. It should be really easy."

"Should we wear masks?" Tony, the oldest of the three Waslala men, asked.

"Aw, I'm not worried about it. There's nobody around."

"I'm wearing one," Tony snapped. "I'm not taking any risks."

"What kind of weapons do we have?" Franklin asked. "How many machetes?"

They had two machetes and two knives. "Okay," Franklin said, taking a deep puff on his cigar. "I'll take a knife. The rest of you guys take a weapon, too. I have my bar along to bust open the door. Are we ready? Let's go!"

The back porch was enclosed in mesh. It didn't take Franklin long at all to jerk out the staples at the base and make an opening large enough for the smallest of their crew. He slipped through and opened the door for the rest. Their flashlights bobbing, they quickly checked what was available in the back porch. "Food!" Franklin gloated, picking out several jars of canned goods from a shelf. "I'm hungry! Let's eat some of this stuff!"

"We'll eat when we're done," Tony growled. "Let's get on with the show."

Franklin's mind was in high gear as he jabbed at the boards on the bottom half of the door. The drugs had done their job. He felt like a giant who could do anything with his tremendous strength and wisdom. Recklessly, he banged and ripped at the boards.

"Shhhhh!" Tony complained. "You're going to wake the whole neighborhood!"

"Ha!" Franklin laughed, "There's no one around. We can be as loud as we want."

The skinny robber slipped into the main part of the house and opened the door from the inside. One robber stayed out on the porch to guard while the rest started searching the kitchen and living room. They were quiet now, hurriedly grabbing whatever loot they could find.

Tony grabbed a computer bag, and Franklin found a decent rechargeable flashlight. Suddenly, the robbers heard a muffled noise and a shout from the bedroom. Someone leaped out of the bed and flipped the living room light on. For a second everyone froze in the bright light—robbers and victim. Franklin recognized Albert Strubhar, the *gringo's* schoolteacher, dressed in his cut-offs, barefoot, jostle-haired, and clearly shocked. The robbers ran, Tony still clinging to the computer bag.

"Let that be!" Albert blurted out.

Tony's large blue handkerchief covered his face, leaving two holes for his eyes. As he ran, he looked around and sassed, "No way!" The computer bag escaped through the open door after its new owner, and Albert groaned. *There go my passports and all my important papers!*

When the robbers regrouped, Tony whispered angrily, "You liar! There *was* someone there after all!"

"I didn't know he was there!" Franklin stammered. "I was sure the house was empty! But why are we out here like scared chickens? I'm not scared of those *gringos!* Let's go get them!" Then, swinging around, Franklin ran back toward the house, the other three robbers following close on his heels.

Franklin stopped when he saw the closed door. Grabbing the machete from Tony, he stuck it through the hole he had made earlier, brandishing it menacingly. "Give me your money!" he barked.

Albert brought some money and handed it out through the hole.

"Open up!" Franklin growled.

Albert opened the door. Looking at the small amount of money Albert had given him, Franklin noticed that some of it was foreign currency. "We don't want any stupid Costa Rican money!" he spit out. "We want good, solid córdobas."

Albert didn't tell him the money they didn't recognize was dollars. He just answered truthfully, "I don't have any more money."

Franklin moved into the bedroom where Albert had been sleeping. Albert followed. There Franklin saw a thin, black, box-like thing lying on the bed.

"What's that?" he asked.

"A machine."

"What kind of a machine?" Franklin insisted. "What's it for?"

Albert's mind was racing. *What can I do? I have all my photos in there. My diaries and letters of my whole courtship, all my school materials, I just can't let it go!*

"I use it to write letters and do my studies. I use it a lot," Albert answered lamely.

"Is it a computer?" Franklin asked.

Albert nodded.

"I'll take it," Franklin announced, reaching for it.

"Please," Albert begged. "It's a very important instrument to me. It won't do you any good. I—"

"Give me five hundred córdobas," Franklin bargained, "and I will leave it."

"I don't have five hundred córdobas," Albert said. "I would have already given it to you when you asked for all my money."

The laptop stayed.

For the next fifteen minutes, the robbers helped themselves to whatever they could find. Franklin was enjoying the fun. It was a little like going into a store where they had things he had never seen before. He could just help himself, and he didn't have to pay!

Albert stood in a daze and watched them. They took his wallet, his Leatherman, his rubber boots, and several sets of keys.

The CD player and all the CDs they could find. Two watches. Albert's cooperation confirmed Franklin's decision to be nice to the *gringo*. Once they were ready to leave, Albert asked Tony if he could get his passport and papers out of the bag.

Tony brought the bag back. He had obviously searched it for money. He finally grunted, "Just keep this thing. It's too complicated for me." Franklin grinned. Albert sighed in relief.

Then Franklin asked about the radios. "Can you call the police with these?" Franklin asked.

"No, I can't," Albert answered. "Plus, I will unplug them so they are useless."

Franklin warned him that if he called the police, there would be trouble. He didn't take the radios.

All at once, Franklin was ready to leave. It was risky to stay longer. They left the house, and Albert followed them. Suddenly, Albert asked Tony, "Could I have my flashlight back? It doesn't have regular batteries. You have to have electricity to charge it. It won't do you any good."

Franklin nodded to Tony, so he gave the flashlight back. Albert thanked them profusely.

Regrouping on the hill, Franklin started out, "There sure wasn't much money, but we have a lot of stuff. I wish I hadn't let that stinker keep his computer."

"You let him keep his computer?" Tony asked, shaking his head. "Man, you are stupid! We forgot the canned goods, too. Why don't you go back?"

Minutes later, Franklin and one of the younger robbers were again entering the front yard. Albert had stepped out into the moonlight to find some of the smaller things the thieves had dropped in their haste. Albert had gathered them into a pile and was just ready to take them inside. But Franklin had other plans. Playing it rough, he advanced to Albert, bent over, and grabbed the small things. A battery charger. Some batteries.

One of the CDs. "The boss says we have to have the computer," he commanded as he straightened.

Albert tried his best to explain how much he needed the laptop, and how it wouldn't work for them anyway, but Franklin insisted. So Albert led him into the house and gave it to him. Albert asked Franklin if he could have the school keys back. He explained that he needed them in the morning to open the school house. Franklin fished the keys out of his pocket. He gave Albert the jeep keys also. But the house keys he kept. *The missionaries will have to change a lot of locks tomorrow,* he grinned. *Or I will have easy access to their stuff!*

While Franklin and Albert were in the house, the young robber helped himself to the canned food.

Finally, Franklin was ready to leave for sure. He strode out of the house and headed for the shadows. He was surprised to hear a soft, *"Que Dios les bendiga."*

The words smote Franklin's conscience. He had been trying hard to be a Christian, but now he was stealing again. Even now, his family and the people at church still thought he was a Christian. Turning quickly, he echoed, "May God bless you, too!"

The robbers devoured one jar of mango sauce, and barely put a dent in the jar of green beans. They hid the jars in the weeds and headed up the road toward Waslala.

Several weeks later, Franklin was at his grandfather's place. He was surprised when a bus stopped in front of his house and a *gringo* jumped off and walked toward the house. His first impulse was to run. *But I can't,* he mused. *If I run, everybody will know I'm guilty.*

The *gringo* was Albert.

Questions raced through Franklin's mind while he and his grandfather visited with Albert. *What does this man want? Does he recognize me? Why didn't I wear a mask the other night like Tony did? How did he find out it was us?*

By the time Albert asked to talk to him privately, Franklin was ready. They stepped outside behind the house, and Albert didn't beat around the bush. "Look, Franklin, you wouldn't happen to know anything about my computer that was stolen recently, would you?"

"No," Franklin answered, too quickly. "Are you blaming me for stealing your computer, or what?"

"No," Albert answered kindly. "It's just they've told me you have connections."

"That's true, but just so you know for sure, I wasn't in your robbery. The day they stole from you, I was in jail," he lied.

"I just thought you might have an idea who stole it and could help me buy it back."

"Yeah, well, I do know who robbed you. It was Black Saint and three boys from Yahoska. I would be willing to go to Yahoska and see what I can do. I would need some money for the bus fare . . ."

"Okay, it's a deal," Albert agreed, fishing a hundred córdobas from his pocket. "If you find anything, let me know."

The two parted as old friends.

Franklin schemed some more. He needed money. He knew Tony's wife had already sold the laptop to a man in Waslala. But he could play the game, he decided. Two days later, he walked up to the Kusulí school house just as classes were over. He called Albert to come outside, and they walked up the road together until they were far from any houses.

"Albert, you have luck. I found your computer," Franklin said in low tones. "The guy has it in Yahoska and is willing to deal. He wants to know how much you would give him."

"Well, the night they stole it, the robber told me that if I came up with five hundred córdobas ($30), I could keep it. But I would actually give double that," Albert admitted, remembering what the laptop had cost him.

Franklin's eyes were shining now. *I got him!* He crowed. "Look, get me a thousand córdobas and I will have the computer here by tomorrow evening."

Albert frowned. "Do I have to give money in advance?"

"Yeah, I guess you do. See, the fellow is a toughie. He won't turn the thing loose until he sees the money."

"Tell him to come personally."

"Oh, never," Franklin groaned, rolling his eyes. "He would never come to Kusulí or meet you. He's the one who stole from you. He can't afford to do that. But, trust me, if you give me the money, I will get you your machine."

"I don't have the money on me," Albert replied. "Let's go on up to Tim's place. He can give me some advice and maybe loan me the money."

As they walked back to Tim's place, Franklin talked a mile a minute. Even as he talked, his mind was spinning. *If he'd had the money, he would have handed it over. But if he talks to Tim, Tim might warn him.*

Trying one more tactic, Franklin added as warmly as he could, "You can trust me now, Albert. It's true that I used to be a robber and I used to smoke marijuana, but since I am a Christian I dropped all that."

"Yeah," Albert responded. "I heard that you went to the *encuentro* and found the Lord. That's the best thing for you to do. Follow Christ. You can make restitution for your evil deeds and go straight. That's where you'll find peace and joy."

"That's so true," Franklin gushed. He could almost feel the thousand córdobas in his pocket. "I really love the Lord now. My testimony is that serving Christ is by far the best life!" Franklin clinched the conversation as Albert turned into Tim's lane.

"I'll meet you up the road a ways," Franklin said, grinning as they parted.

Franklin waited impatiently. What was taking Albert so long? Surely Tim would not kill his plan!

Finally, Albert showed up, and they walked up the road around the corner. Albert began to speak slowly. "I asked Tim for advice. I even called Pablo from Waslala on the radio, and they both suggested that I not give you money."

"But why not? You can trust me."

"It is best to give the money once the computer is in our hands, that's all. Maybe you are honest, but that other man is a robber, and he could just keep the money and the computer. Robbers are that way, as you know."

Franklin was stumped. His thoughts raced during the silence between them. *They got me. I am the robber. I would have pulled his leg. I missed a thousand córdobas that time.*

Albert's thoughts ran differently. *I wish I knew if this guy is for real. Pablo even recommended that I not meet him at a place alone, and here I am. He reminded me that he has killed for money. But what if he is a Christian? He talks nice. But I will stick with what my advisers say.*

"What shall we do then?" Franklin asked.

"Take one hundred córdobas so you can prove to the man that this is serious. Tell him you will take the computer and be back the next day with the money. That's all I can offer."

Albert handed Franklin the money, and Franklin was gone. Albert never saw him again.

Two weeks later, a Waslala lawyer walked up to Albert's friend and asked. "Have any of you lost a laptop?"

"My friend Albert did," the friend answered.

"A week ago, a lady came and offered me a laptop. It did not have a charger and the battery was dead. Suspecting that it was stolen, I gave her a little money and told her to come back once I located a cord to charge it. I finally found one and started it up. The main user is blocked by a password, but the visitor's account opened right up, and some of the first things I found were photos of your people. Then I knew it was stolen. Tell Albert to come and get his laptop."

That same afternoon, at the lawyer's place, Albert popped in his password and his account opened immediately. Albert's grin was a delight to see. Everything in the computer was intact. When he tried to offer the lawyer money, the lawyer asked, "How can I charge you to get your own computer back? I bought a stolen item; I lose the money."

Albert insisted, and the lawyer finally accepted the amount he had given Tony's wife. And when she came around to ask for the rest of the money, she went home with a lecture instead.

One evening, two young men were drinking in one of Waslala's bars, half a dozen empty beer bottles on the table between them. "Like I was telling you," Franklin burped, "I really give those *gringos* a hard time. It's so easy to steal from them."

"But they are nice people," Carlos insisted. "I have worked for Pablo off and on, and my uncle has worked for him for six years."

"Hey, they say—hic—they say that Pablo guy is really easy to steal from. They used to rob him with anything from a corn cob to a green banana—hic—but he moved away a few years ago."

"He was chased away," Carlos corrected his drunken friend.

"Well, whatever," Franklin said. "I don't care why they moved to Waslala. I just wish they lived back in Kusulí yet. Then I could have a chance at him, too." Franklin roared with laughter.

"I don't think it's funny," Carlos insisted.

"Well, at least Tim's around yet. I've gotten into his house before. And I'm brave enough to do it again, anytime."

Several months later, Manuel, a cousin of Franklin's, came to Waslala to visit. The cousin lived with his family way back in El Plátano. Manuel's dad, a Catholic, didn't get along with his evangelical family from Waslala, so there was very little contact between the family members.

Manuel told Franklin that the news about him killing the two men had reached all the way to El Plátano, and claimed he was worried for him.

"Look, Franklin, your life is in danger," Manuel connived. "We have heard rumors that Santiago's family is planning to come and get you here. I came to warn you. You need to run. Come to El Plátano with me and you will be safe. We live more than seven hours from Waslala, and no one will find you there. We can loan you land to plant. We will be friends."

So Franklin moved to El Plátano. Time ticked on, and the pieces of a malevolent plan fell into place. Franklin was as good as dead.

The sun was hot. There was no breeze, and the air seemed thick and oppressive. Franklin and Manuel planted beans lazily—a small step with the left foot, then a jab in the soft soil with the metal-tipped stick, making a little hole. Drop in three bean seeds with the left hand. Close the hole with a quick tamp with the right foot, then another step.

"I'd like to go back to Waslala," Franklin said. "I miss my family."

"No, you don't want to go back to Waslala," Manuel answered. "You're better off here with us. You can work and stay out of trouble. It's only been two months."

It's true, Franklin mused. *Maybe it is better if I stay here with my uncle. I don't get in trouble as much. If I were in Waslala, I would be stealing.*

Franklin and Manuel topped the rise, still planting beans. Just over the ridge was a little grove of trees. Walking toward them from the grove were two men. One carried a gun. Franklin froze, the blood draining from his heart. *This is it,* he realized.

"They're after you!" Manuel gulped, acting surprised.

Franklin wheeled and fled over the rise. *Bang!* The gun spoke once. Franklin stumbled and fell as the bullet ripped into his hip. Manuel fled across the bean field, down over the hill, and on home. The armed men ran up to confront their enemy, now bleeding among the bean seeds he had planted earlier.

Few people will ever know what happened during the last hour of Franklin's life. His two enemies know. Franklin himself knows. But since dead men don't speak, he's not likely to tell.

But several people have a good idea what happened. They know some of the hideous details.

Franklin's uncle and cousins went to find him that afternoon after they were sure the armed men had left. It wasn't hard to find the place where they had shot him. There was plenty of blood to mark that spot, but it took them a long time to locate his body. Just before dark they found him, buried under a pile of dead leaves and sticks in the little stand of jungle where the men had been hiding, waiting to execute their attack. When they pulled him out from under the leaves, Franklin's body told the story.

They found the bullet hole where they had shot him as he ran. But that hadn't killed him. They found a section of his chest and part of his leg where the bloodthirsty men had literally cut and ripped the skin off his body. As the men stood there shaking their heads, one of them shuddered and said, "When they skinned him, he was still alive!"

After the torture, they cut off Franklin's head. The scene was so horrible that the relatives trembled. They decided to look for the head and then report to the nearest police station before retrieving the body. They searched until it got too dark to continue. They didn't find it. Not that evening. Not the next day when the police came. Nor a week later when the buzzards could have helped. But they did find something that made the story even more awful. At the scene of Franklin's torture, they found his tongue.

The reason they didn't find the head, they discovered later, was that Franklin's enemies had carried the head in a sack back to Dipina where Santiago awaited the prize. The head was proof that the avengers had done their job.

Can you imagine what thoughts raced through Franklin's mind as he was tortured that last hour of his life? What was he screaming when they skinned him alive? Then did the screams turned into a raspy roar as his tongue was cut out? Did his mind go right on remembering, even as his life's blood drained from his body?

Why did I not seek God? Why did I not repent? Why did I enjoy my wicked ways? Here I am, only seventeen years old, already paying for my sins. I wasted all my opportunities. Now I am doomed forever . . .

Did his stealing episodes race like a movie through his mind? Marijuana? Deer, chickens, and *guardiolas*? Frightened men, women, and children? The scene when he shot two men for money? Prison? The times the missionaries had showered love upon him and witnessed to him? The times he had sought God and felt a touch of His love? His public confession?

I don't know what all Franklin thought as he was dying, but I know it had to be terrible. Yet it was nothing compared to what he faced after he died and met the Master!

Chapter Three
A BLASPHEMER'S PAY

The night was dark and humid. The waning moon hid its face behind a bank of black clouds. Two young men sat on the hillside swatting mosquitoes. Roberto asked his older brother, "Why don't we just go down and get it over with? It's getting late. Before long, they will be asleep. Or are you scared?"

"Have patience," Marcos answered tersely, caressing the twenty-two he held across his knees. "We need to time things just right. I don't think these *gringos* will be violent, but we need to be careful. They don't own guns," he added, though without confidence.

The thatched-roof, bamboo-walled house below them loomed dark on the slope. Many cracks in the walls allowed the candlelight to filter through, making the house resemble a zebra with funny yellow stripes. In the house lived a young couple of *gringos* who had recently moved into the area. Roberto had heard they were missionaries planning to start a church. He had seen them from a distance several times, but had never actually talked to them.

"Do you think they will understand you?" Roberto asked Marcos.

"They know Spanish," Marcos answered. "I met the preacher the other day, and we visited. He speaks Spanish fluently. Let's go on down and see if these *gringos* have any money."

The two robbers approached the house. They could hear the young couple conversing in another language right inside the wall. Roberto was nervous, yet he felt a wild thrill of exhilaration. But Marcos was not so excited. Though he had been involved in many robberies before, he was almost sorry he had suggested this robbery to his daredevil, teenage brother. Now that it was time to speak up, his mouth was dry, and he trembled slightly. He intentionally shuffled his feet as he walked up to the door. [10]

Immediately the voices within hushed to whispers. Roberto watched to see what Marcos would do. Would he holler to make them open up, or would they have to kick the door down like they did at the natives' homes?

They didn't have long to wait. They heard a rustle inside, then the door opened and a tall man stepped into the doorway and shone his flashlight right into their faces. Roberto stood half-sheltered behind Marcos, but he could see that the *gringo's* boldness scared Marcos. With a tremor in his voice, Marcos barked, "Come out here and cut that flashlight off!"

The *gringo* obeyed, lowered his light, and stepped right up to Marcos. "Give me your flashlight," Marcos ordered.

The *gringo* handed it over.

"We need money," Marcos stammered. "We want fifteen hundred dollars!"

"I'm sorry. I don't have any dollars," the man told them kindly. "I don't carry much money. I do happen to have 900 córdobas ($100) on me that I brought from Waslala to pay for a load of block and sand that never came. I can give you that."

"I don't believe you!" Marcos grumbled. "Go bring your money."

10 The missionaries' side of the story can be found in Angels Over Waslala, Chapter 20.

"I don't lie because I am a Christian," the *gringo* continued. "If you don't believe me, search my house."

"Bring me your billfold then," Marcos commanded.

When the *gringo* returned with his billfold, he handed it to Marcos and asked, "May I have my license and other important papers?"

Marcos squatted down and emptied the billfold's contents onto the ground. Roberto wondered what was wrong with his tough brother. He would have refused to be intimidated by the *gringo* and would have grabbed the stuff and run. But Marcos was actually being nice. After giving everything back except the billfold and the money, Marcos continued. "Give me your radio."

"Which one?" the *gringo* asked.

"Oh," Roberto muttered, "he has more than one radio. That's great!"

"How many do you have?" Marcos asked.

"Two. One big one and another small one."

"I'll take the small one."

After the *gringo* came back with the radio, the robber took it and barked, "Now get inside."

The *gringo* closed the door slowly. Marcos and Roberto ran up the hill in the direction they had come. Before going too far, Marcos stopped and hissed back toward the cabin, "Blow out the candles!"

Nothing happened.

"Blow out those candles!" Marcos snapped, a little louder.

Catching on, the *gringo* called out, "Sure! I'm sorry. I didn't understand you the first time."

Marcos softened and shouted back, "Don't worry. We won't hurt you people. It's just that we needed money."

———————————

A dark pall had settled over the whole Kusulí community. The news spread like wildfire. "Charro and a hundred and fifty of his men are setting up camp in the valley by the Unida church house." The name struck fear into every heart for miles around.

Roberto and Marcos heard the news toward evening. "Let's lay low and stay at home tonight," Marcos suggested. "Tomorrow we will wait to leave the house until we hear they've left." Roberto knew his brother spoke wisely.

The next morning at seven, Don Pancho was sitting in the Assemblies of God church house, waiting for the rest of the brethren to join him for a day of prayer and fasting. He had just settled down on a bench when one of his daughters came running into the church house, panting, and gasped, "Daddy, they took Marcos and Roberto!"

"Who took whom?" Don Pancho asked slowly.

"Charro's men took them. Just a bit ago. They just walked into the house carrying machine guns and said, 'Marcos and Roberto, ¡vámosnos! (Let's go!)' The boys didn't say a word; they just stared at the guns and obeyed. Mom is at home weeping. Please, Daddy, do something!"

Don Pancho had been a wicked man in his day. Born and raised in the Matagalpa area, he had moved his family to Waslala when he was forty years old. Though Don Pancho had been a staunch Catholic, he had lived a brazen life of sin. He drank, gambled, supervised cockfights, and fought other men who drank like he did.

One day, tired of all his problems, he attended a church service at his neighbor's place. After the message, Don Pancho walked up to the pulpit and announced, "Pray for me. I am going to try my best to be a Christian."

After that, Don Pancho was a changed man. All over the Kusulí hills the story was repeated, "Don Pancho was converted. He doesn't drink or gamble anymore."

Don Pancho married his live-in companion. His wife accepted Christ three months later. Together they went to church and tried to raise their eleven children for the Lord. Things seemed to go well for a while, but as time went on, it became obvious that some of Don Pancho's sons would not follow in their father's footsteps. Marcos, his sixth son, was an angry, bitter young man. Roberto, the next younger, imitated him. A friend of theirs began taking them into Waslala and inducing them to drink. He also taught them to steal. Don Pancho and his wife heard rumors of their boys' wicked ways.

Then Marcos and Roberto made a serious mistake. They started hanging around the infamous Doña Amparo. Everyone knew she was Charro's mistress and a wicked woman not to be trifled with. Marcos and Roberto frequented her place and drank with her and her friends. They also stole for her. They became her agents. Whenever Charro came around, they ran and hid.

Don Pancho pleaded with his boys about their dangerous behavior. Marcos only got angry. "Don't mess with my life," he'd fuss at his father. "You mind your business, and I'll mind mine!"

"But, son," Don Pancho admonished, "I know you are stealing. That Amparo woman is not good company. You will get into trouble if you hang around her."

Roberto didn't get angry at his father like Marcos did, but he didn't listen either. He just laughed at his dad and at sin.

Then one day, the two boys convinced Doña Amparo's two girls to go for a walk with them. When the girls refused to go farther, Roberto grabbed one girl by the hand and Marcos grabbed the other. They started to drag them away by force. The girls screamed and Amparo heard them. She came running and saw it all. The boys ran home.

So when Charro stopped with his men to pick up Marcos and Roberto, everyone knew those two young men were doomed.

Don Pancho stopped his horse and surveyed the tree-studded valley before him. Charro and one hundred and fifty men had camped in the Dudú valley. Smoke from several fires created pillars of gray among the trees. Everywhere, armed men scurried, busily stoking fires and butchering. Charro had bought a steer, and his men were cooking up a storm.

Two days had passed since Charro had taken Marcos and Roberto. Their father had followed them and now he prepared to negotiate with Charro. As soon as Don Pancho topped the mountain, a watchman saw him. Holding his machine gun tightly, the guard snapped, "What are you doing here?"

"I am Don Pancho, and I have come to talk with Charro. He is holding two of my sons hostage, and I want to see what we can work out."

"Follow me."

The soldiers barely noticed the farmer riding among them. They were used to mingling with the back-country people, and they were too hungry for distractions. They cut the meat into thin strips and hung it over the fire, where big kettles of yucca also boiled. Some of the men were eating the meat half raw. The guard led Don Pancho across a gully to the house of a farmer who had befriended the guerillas. The guard called out, "Charro, there is someone here who wants to talk with you."

"Tell him to come in," a deep voice boomed.

Don Pancho dismounted and strode into the shabby, thatched-roof house. Squinting in the semi-darkness, Don Pancho saw Charro sitting at a table. He was a tall, slim, white-skinned man. Some said he looked like a *gringo*. He had studied at West Point in the United States and had been trained for guerilla warfare in Honduras. He wore a long, brown beard and had a bandanna tied around his forehead. He was sitting back in his chair, plate empty, sipping a cup of black coffee through an impressively large mustache.

Don Pancho had met Charro on different occasions, so he walked across the dirt floor and shook his hand. After a minute or two of friendly conversation, Charro got to the point.

"What can I do for you?"

"My boys. You have them, right?"

"I have one. Commandant Zapoyal has the other. We are trying to shape them into real soldiers."

Don Pancho sighed. At least they were still alive. "I would appreciate it if you would let me have my sons back."

"You know they are wicked?" Charro asked, his eyes narrowing into slits. "They are robbers. They tried to rape Amparo's daughters. Why should I turn them loose?"

"What you are saying is true. They are wicked boys, and they don't deserve to live. But what if I made myself responsible for them? Especially Roberto, he's only fifteen."

"I had heard that these boys were stealing with the Berlines (an infamous robber band). I know now that's not true. But they are robbers, and we want to avoid any more trouble."

"I will do what I can," Don Pancho said humbly.

"Go, call Marcos in," Charro boomed to one of his men. Soon Marcos strode in. He grinned when he saw his dad. Charro began. "Marcos, have I done anything bad against you? Have I beaten you? Have I touched a hair on your head?"

"No. You have treated me well. I might stay and be part of your group."

"That's what I was hoping," Charro said. "Have you had enough to eat?"

"Yes."

"Has anybody been mistreating you?"

"No."

Turning to Don Pancho, Charro continued. "As I was saying, we are trying to reform Marcos. He's learning. If I turn him loose, will he not go back to his old ways? Take him aside and give him some good advice."

Don Pancho led his son out under a nearby tree. There he gave him a lecture like he'd never given Marcos before. Charro's men brought each of them a banana leaf loaded with a big chunk of simmering meat buried under pieces of white yucca. They also brought them each a cup of coffee.

"They treat us well here, as long as we behave. It's not too bad to live with them, really," Marcos assured his father. As his dad warned him and pleaded with him, he just hung his head and listened sullenly. He didn't get angry and argue back like he usually did. Then Don Pancho asked about Roberto.

"They took him to another group led by Zapoyal. I haven't heard a thing about him since."

"They claim they haven't killed him," Don Pancho mused. "I sure hope he's all right. What are you planning, son?"

"I'm going to cooperate so maybe they will let me go."

"What will you do then?"

"That's none of your business!"

When Don Pancho was ready to leave, Charro promised to turn the boys loose. "Bring the minister of your church and their mother. I will warn the boys in your presence and let you take them. They will then be responsible to you. But Lord have mercy if they steal again!"

It had rained all night. The hammock was strung between two trees, and the highest branches groaned in the wind. Roberto shivered under his thin blanket. He was sick. He was sure he was going to die. If the guerrillas didn't kill him, his sickness would. The fever that was burning up his body was also affecting his brain.

I'm glad they gave me plastic to drape over my hammock, or I would be drenched in this rain. I wonder what Zapoyal will do with me tomorrow. Will he cut my throat like he does the other robbers he catches?

It had been three days since Charro's men had picked up Roberto at his home. His initial terror was past. The first day he had been sure they would kill him. Now his fear was waning. Plus, there was a rumor that his father had come to Charro and pleaded for them. *That's just like my old man,* Roberto mused. *I wonder what he thinks of us now and what he told Charro. Maybe Charro will turn us loose. Or let us be soldiers in his army. That would be better than having my throat cut.* Roberto shivered in his hammock and longed for morning.

The next morning, he was too sick to walk, but it was time to move on. When Charro's doctor came to give him medicine for his fever, Roberto noted how kind he was. He was dressed just like the other soldiers, in common clothes with leather army boots. Just like the rest, his clothes stank of old sweat and mold. The rain was taking its toll on the whole group. Everyone seemed discouraged and longed for the sun to come out and dry things a little.

After taking his medicine and drinking a mug of black coffee, Roberto was surprised to see a soldier leading a horse toward him. The guerrillas didn't have many horses, and they were mainly used to haul cargo. Yet, somehow they produced a horse with a saddle, and Roberto rode.

The rain had stopped by evening when they arrived at their next camping place. Roberto felt a little better, but after a quick supper, he crawled into his hammock. There his dreams and troubled thoughts continued. *If I ever get out of here, I will respect my dad,* he vowed. *I will be good and work like my dad always wanted me to. I will make a change in my life, and someday my dad will be proud of me. I wonder if I will have another chance . . .*

Three weeks later, the guerrillas camped close to Waslala. Knowing the army might try to attack, they tried their best to set up camp in silence. Roberto was so tired he strung up his hammock before they passed the cold food around. No one could cook this close to Waslala.

Right after they ate, Zapoyal walked over to him and snapped, "You are going with us tonight!"

"Where are we going?" Roberto asked.

"That's none of your business. Let's go."

Roberto joined a small group of men gathering outside the camp. Zapoyal was talking with Charro by radio, and Roberto could hear their plan to meet that night. Soon a group of seven was marching through the fields in the pitch dark toward Waslala. Zapoyal and two of his big shots were in the lead. Three bodyguards and Roberto made up the rest of the group.

When they arrived at the road from El Caño de los Martínez to Waslala, Zapoyal hissed, "Quiet now, boys! We don't need any run-ins with the law right now. That would really throw a wrench in our political plans. We can't afford any trouble. Roberto, you try any tricks and you are a dead man, got it?"

The seven men slipped silently through the fence and took to the road. Immediately, they heard the mournful call of a nighthawk. For a moment, Roberto was afraid, but then Zapoyal answered with a song so authentic that Roberto almost looked around to see the bird.

The two nighthawks continued to call back and forth until they met. Another group of men crawled through the fence and onto the road. Roberto's eyes strained to see in the darkness. Right away he recognized Charro himself, surrounded by bodyguards. Roberto tried his best to find Marcos among the men, but he was disappointed. Marcos was not with them.

Just before entering town, the silent group left the road and walked through the fields. Soon they were walking along the shores of the Waslala River. This approach into town was fairly safe. There were no houses close to the shoreline, and at that time of the night no one was out by the river. When they came near a house, the men waded into the shallow water's edge.

At lonely places, they walked up on the banks to make better time.

Suddenly, Charro made the sound of the nighthawk, and they left the river and sneaked toward town. They walked up an alley, single file, the bodyguards ready with their machine guns. The leaders walked in the middle of the line. Roberto walked in front of them.

Roberto saw a big, red building looming ahead in the middle of a grassy lot. Lights were on inside, and the door shone like gold in the dark night. He recognized the place immediately, and gasped. *Pantaleón's furniture shop! What in the world are we doing here?* The building had been an old German's carpentry shop before he was gunned down by the guerrillas. Now a native Waslalan rented the building with the tools. *What could Charro want in the carpenter's shop at this hour?* Roberto wondered.

Zapoyal went inside by himself. The rest hid in the shadows. Soon he came back and hissed, "All's well."

Charro entered first, a bodyguard on either side. Roberto was next, moving cautiously. To his surprise, several people were already sitting around a table. This was obviously a political meeting. Charro walked over to the group and shook hands with Carlos Pinto, a short little Brazilian priest known for his leftist leanings. Next, he shook hands with the head of police, who had rightist leanings. Several others of Waslala's important citizens were in the group. The army leaders, with strong leftist leanings, were obviously not invited. Soon Charro was laughing and talking and helping himself to the case of beer on the table.

Roberto's eyes wandered toward the back of the building. It was darker there, and Roberto saw a huddle of people. Tears sprang to his eyes when he saw his mother and father. And there was Tirso, his dad's minister. Then Charro shouted, *"Don*

Pancho, acércate. Vamos a salir con lo tuyo primero (Don Pancho, step up. We're going to take care of your deal first)."

Charro indicated the three who had come to intercede for Roberto. Roberto was touched to see how much his family loved him and how they had to come so far to rescue him. They had even brought the preacher along. Charro ordered Roberto to sit in the center of the circle, and the meeting began. The priest and the other Waslala representatives were there as silent witnesses.

Charro's eyes were glued to Roberto's face. "The reason I am giving you another chance, Son, is because I have hope for you. I want you to obey your father. He is a good man. If you do that, you will change and make a man out of yourself. This is your chance. If I find out you are back on the bad road, you are a dead man. Do you understand? Especially if you steal, I will track you down."

Roberto nodded.

Next, Charro talked to Roberto's parents and the preacher, explaining their duty. On the basis of these agreements, he announced, "I allow Roberto to go home to behave himself and become a man."

Then, turning to Don Pancho, Charro continued. "I'm sorry I don't have Marcos for you tonight, but he sneaked away and deserted. I plan to catch him again; then I will bring him and turn him back over to you."

After Roberto's release, the men gathered around the table for their political meeting. Roberto followed his father and mother out into the darkness. He had never loved his family as he loved them that night.

Soon after Roberto came home, a soldier who had deserted from Charro's group stopped by and told Don Pancho and Roberto the truth about Marcos. "One day he got into a fight with one of Charro's top guys. He grabbed a stick and hit the commander over the head. He was trying to get his gun away from him. If he had, there would have been a shootout. That Marcos had a terrible temper." The soldier shook his head. "The commander hollered and told Charro what Marcos had done. Charro hollered back, 'Kill the rat!' So they did. They dug a shallow grave and buried him in the jungle."

For several years, Roberto tried to avoid trouble. He moved in with a girl, and she seemed to help him straighten up. He worked with his dad, and their business thrived. He traveled into remote areas and bought corn and beans at reasonable prices and shipped them out, selling them for a profit.

During that time, Charro was killed and his group disintegrated. Any influence his threats might have had on Roberto died with him.

Years passed. Roberto left his first woman and moved in with another one from Puerto Cabezas, a port town on the east coast. After some time, they moved to the coast, a two-day ride by bus. In Puerto Cabezas, Roberto's life went awry again. His woman drew him into drugs and drinking. With that came stealing. But by far the worst thing he got involved in was witchcraft. He could never forget what had happened to his brother Marcos, and he wanted to be sure that it would never happen to him. So he made a pact with the devil for protection. In the pact, the devil promised that Roberto could never die.

As time went on, Roberto became good friends with the *gringos*. Pablo especially liked his friendly ways and big smile. After Roberto came back from the coast, he attended a burial. Pablo was in charge of the service, and afterward he singled Roberto out to witness to him. But when Pablo warned him about what could happen if he was not ready to die, he just laughed it off. For Roberto, nothing was serious anymore—not even death.

Back at home, even though Roberto had learned to work with cattle, he soon discovered that stealing cattle was an easier way to make quick cash. In the evening, he and his youngest brother, Alfredo, would snatch an animal from someone's herd and run it all night to Sofana. There they would sell the cow and then steal another one to take back and sell in Waslala.

Don Pancho was disgusted with his son. He didn't work on the farm at all anymore. And the more his father scolded him, the less Roberto came home.

Roberto turned into an arrogant, wild, wicked man. Everyone knew he was a thief. He didn't care. He stole anyway, and soon the few friends he had turned against him.

Roberto had come to respect the *gringos* over the years and knew they were friendly. Pablo had moved to the town of Waslala. Tim, the man who was now the leader of the church in Kusulí, had some Holstein heifers. Roberto knew these would make good money in Sofana,. And the *gringos* didn't get you in trouble with the law. They just prayed for you.

The more Roberto thought about stealing and selling Holstein heifers, the better he liked the idea. Alfredo was ready, too. A friend of theirs, called Ródrigo, had joined their band. They were now a real robber band, and Alfredo was fast becoming the worst of them all.

The stars were bright and clear that night. Three young men approached Tim Schrock's farm from the back, walking stealthily through weedy fields. They covered their flashlights with their hands, allowing only slivers of light to slip through when they chose.

Arriving at Tim's fence, they clipped the wires and stood on the hilltop until they were sure no one else was roaming the area. It was ten o'clock, late enough that no prowlers were apt to be around, and early enough that, by daylight, they would be far, far away.

A dog barked in the distance. The sound came from the farmstead that used to be Pablo's, but now was owned by Don Tacho, a native farmer who owned three guns and a pack of mad dogs. Roberto grinned. *We'd better be glad we're stealing Tim's heifer and not Don Tacho's. This is so much easier. Anyway, Tim's artificially inseminated heifers are worth three times as much as Don Tacho's.*

A rooster crowed somewhere off behind them. "Let's go," Alfredo commanded. "It's getting late."

The dry cows and heifers were lying in the next field, out in the open. The three men crept toward the herd. "If we scare these cows, we'll have a stampede. Let's work quietly, and all will go well."

Roberto eased up to a nice heifer and slipped a rope over her neck. "This is so easy!" he exclaimed. "These critters are as tame as kittens!"

The heifer was halter-broken, and she followed the men easily all night long. By morning, they were close to Sofana. By the end of the next day, they had sold the heifer for a good price and were wondering what to steal for their trip home.

Roberto was riding a large bay mare he had bought with the money from his cow sales. As he rode through Waslala, just after the big bridge, he met his friend, Jaime Chavarría, another cowboy. They pulled off to the side of the cobblestone street to talk, each man slouched on his horse. Roberto knew Jaime had become a Christian and joined the *gringo's* church in Kusulí. He had seen the drastic change in his life and often thought about making a turn in his own life like Jaime had. Usually, however, it was only a passing thought.

Now, sitting on their horses in the sunshine, Roberto and Jaime were talking about cattle prices. Looking up, Roberto saw Pablo approaching, so he prepared himself. *That guy will want to talk to me about God.*

Sure enough, Pablo stopped on the cobblestones and greeted each of the men. Roberto liked the preacher's friendly manner and soon was trying to outwit him as they visited and joked. Then, just as he'd feared, the conversation turned serious. "Roberto, what are you going to do with your life? When are you going to follow Jaime's example and give your heart to the Lord? Do you see how he has changed since he was converted?"

"Yeah," Roberto joked, "he's changed a lot—from bad to worse!"

"You know better than that. He used to be a lot like you, but now he follows the Lord. That's what you need to do, Roberto. You always wear that happy smile, but you don't have a happy heart. You need a heart to match your smile."

Roberto tried again. "Pshaw, I'm a happy man. I'm a good boy. I don't do anything bad."

"Let's be serious, Roberto. I want to tell you a story. Do you remember Carlos Picudo?"

"Of course! We all knew him."

"He was proud and would not listen to God. One day I witnessed to him. I warned him that he was playing games with God. I reminded him that God had tried three times to get his attention. The first time, he had a motorcycle wreck and almost got killed. The next time, he got extremely sick and was in the hospital in terrible shape. I went to visit him. Then, the last time, he got shot in a brawl and had his arm in a sling. I told him he had better listen to God. I warned him that God had given him three small knocks with His left fist to get his attention. Then I asked him, 'Carlos, what will you do when the Lord knocks you over with His right fist?'

"Carlos just laughed and changed the subject. Three months later, they shot him to death. Do you think he thinks about that in hell? Do you think he laughs now?"

Just like Carlos, Roberto laughed. "You get a little carried away, preacher. I'm not going to die yet. Why would the good Lord want to knock me over like that? I'm a good man!"

"Jaime," the preacher asked the other rider, "what can we do to wake this fellow up? His life is in danger. I know God is speaking to him."

"I guess all we can do is warn him and pray for him," Jaime answered. "I constantly tell him things like that too, but he just laughs. He thinks he'll live forever."

Roberto was surprised when Pablo reached up and patted his leg. "Roberto, please remember, God loves you, and we do, too. We really want you to change your ways and find the Lord."

"Someday. Someday, Pablo. Then I'll be a Christian just like you . . ."

———————————

Three months later, Don Pancho sat on his porch in his old rocking chair, tired and discouraged. A neighbor had just stopped by and relayed the latest news about his two sons. They had stolen a cow from a young man in Kusulí. The whole town had been enraged, and several armed men had tracked them down to Sofana. There they caught them red-handed with the cow. Alfredo and Ródrigo were resting beside the road, watching the cow. Roberto was over at the store, drinking beer and trying to sell the cow to the owner. The angry men held them up at gunpoint, cursing and threatening to shoot them on the spot.

In his fear, Roberto confessed that he had stolen heifers from Tim Schrock. Among many other promises, he promised to never steal cattle again.

The angry men finally turned the robbers loose, took the cow, and returned home. They warned Roberto's band that if they ever stole again, they would take matters into their own hands, and then they would definitely never steal again.

Don Pancho knew Roberto was going too far, so he had sent word for Roberto to come to talk with him. Waiting for his son's arrival, he sat in his chair and prayed for the right words. *What can I tell my wicked son?*

Roberto obeyed his dad's summons. He rode up on his horse and joined him on the porch. His mother came out and sat with them. Again, Don Pancho pleaded with his son. He warned him. He witnessed to him. He offered to help him by setting up a deal where he'd buy some heifers and they could raise them on shares. Roberto wouldn't have to produce any money up front. Don Pancho would provide the pasture. "Look, son, I am ashamed of all the rumors. It's hard on me to hear that you are a robber and so bold about it. You are drinking more than ever. You have to change, son. I will help you."

Roberto hung his head.

"What do you say?" his father insisted.

"Yeah, it's a good idea," Roberto answered lamely. "I'll take you up on it. Set it up. I'll cooperate."

But Roberto never came around to start the deal, and Don Pancho learned that his son was drinking worse than ever. He'd ride up and down the Kusulí road, cursing and challenging everyone at the top of his voice—especially the four men who had tracked him down and threatened him. And he kept right on stealing.

One moonlit evening two weeks later, in a little shack lit only by several candles, a young woman had just put two little boys to bed when she heard the dog barking out toward the road. *It must be Roberto,* she guessed, making her way to the door and opening up for her husband. He rushed into the room, gasping, pale as a sheet.

"What happened?" his wife asked.

Roberto was dripping with sweat as if he had run miles. He staggered into the bedroom, looking around as if afraid someone would grab him. Sinking onto the bed, he told his wife a horrible story. "I just had a fight with the devil!"

"What do you mean? Are you drunk again?" his wife inquired, shaken by his strange words.

"No. I am perfectly sober. I was walking home in the moonlight and didn't have a flashlight. I heard something following me. I was scared, so I started walking faster. Whatever was following me sped up too," Roberto groaned.

"What happened then?" his wife pressed.

"Whatever it was grabbed me from behind. I almost died of fright. I was sure it was one of my enemies. Perhaps it was Pedro, the man I hate and have fought many a time. So I swung around to beat the life out him. But the thing was so strong I didn't have a chance!" Roberto shivered. "It was terrible! I went at the guy with my fists, like you know I can. But he started beating me too. He was much stronger. So we grappled at each other front to front. He was not only stronger; he was evil. He paralyzed me. Suddenly all the fight went out of me. I was as weak as a baby. Then, as he thrust me aside, I got a good look at him in the moonlight. He was a lot taller than I am. He was black, and his face was indescribable. I fell on the side of the road and he disappeared. I lay there for at least half an hour, terrified, until my strength came back. I still hurt all over from the beating he gave me."

"Do you think it was Pedro?"

"No! Pedro is not that tall. Plus, he looked black. No human I know even begins to look like him."

"Who do you think it was?" his wife whispered.

"I told you it was the devil. I know it was!" Roberto almost shouted. But shouting didn't make him braver. He still trembled all over. Then he gasped, "I have to go to the saloon for a drink. I'll be right back."

Roberto's wife opened the door for him again. As she watched his silhouette disappear into the darkness, she knew it would be morning before he came back home.

A week later, Don Pancho was out picking cacao pods. As he worked, he thought about his wayward sons. He felt better since he had warned Roberto and pleaded with him. He had done all he could. He pondered his dream of several nights before. Was it a premonition?

Don Pancho heard a shuffle among the dry cacao leaves. Turning toward the sound, he saw two men walking toward him. To his surprise, it was his two sons, Roberto and Alfredo. They greeted him and hunched down, leaning against the cacao trees. Don Pancho waited.

Roberto began. "Alfredo wants to change."

"Wants to what?" Don Pancho asked, surprised.

"He wants to be a Christian," Roberto snickered.

Don Pancho looked at Alfredo to see if there was any evidence on his face, but Alfredo's wicked grin told him immediately that it was all an ugly joke.

"Boys," Don Pancho exhorted, shaking his head, "you are playing with God. You are going to get in trouble."

"Yeah," Alfredo joked, "they're saying they're going to kill Roberto here."

Roberto leaped to his feet. "Who's saying that?" he challenged, pointing an angry finger at his brother.

"Ah, don't get so shook up, brother. It doesn't mean it's going to happen."

"I want to know who is saying that. Tell me right now!"

"I'm not telling you. Besides, you always say no one can kill you. Why are you so scared now?"

"I'm not scared. I just want to know who has the nerve to say things like that. No one can kill me! I cannot die!" he almost shouted. Then he burst out laughing.

Don Pancho stared in horror. The wind rustled the upper cacao leaves. Very soberly he spoke. "Roberto, I had a dream the other night. It was an awful dream. I think it's from the Lord."

"What did you dream, Father, dear?" Roberto mocked.

"A man was very angry at you. He was jealous of his wife. In the dream, he killed you. Son, I think God is warning you. If you don't listen, I am afraid the dream will come true."

"Oh, Dad, no one is going to kill me. I'm not stealing anybody's wife. I'm a good boy, right, Alfredo? I'm 'bout like an angel."

Don Pancho scanned Alfredo's face. A knowing look flashed across it. Did he know the man in the dream? Did he know who Roberto was flirting with, and which husband was threatening to kill him? Don Pancho shook his head again and said, "Boys, I have warned you many times. There is nothing more I can do."

Suddenly, the boys were ready to leave. As they walked back toward Kusulí, Alfredo told Roberto, "Hey, do you want to know who's threatening to kill you? It's Pedro."

The very next day, March 25, 2007, dawned bright and clear. Many hearts in Kusulí were happy that morning. But Roberto was furious. He wanted to challenge Pedro for threatening to kill him. So he went to the saloon and got roaring drunk.

Pedro was a young man about Roberto's age. The two boys had grown up neighbors, playing and running around together. Pedro was a tad taller than Roberto, but Roberto was older and wirier. Even in their friendlier days, there had been an underlying competition, and they'd often gotten into fights. Roberto always bragged, "I've fought with Pedro eight times, and I beat him every time!"

But now things were different. Pedro and Roberto weren't boys anymore. They were men. And Roberto was paying Pedro's wife too much attention. Pedro's smoldering anger was ready to burst into flame.

The sun shone brightly that Saturday morning. No one knew what was about to happen—except Roberto. This was the day he would confront his enemy and beat him up for the ninth time.

Pedro had just entered his mother-in-law's house, right across the road from his own home in Kusulí, after sneaking a puff of marijuana out in the banana patch behind the house. His wife was helping her mother cook lunch. Smells of crisply fried tortillas and refried beans stirred his appetite. Pedro's children played on the dirt floor.

Pedro heard shouts. He stepped to the door and looked out. Roberto was staggering up the road, drunk and shouting obscenities as usual.

"Pedro, you bragger, where are you? I hear you're saying you're going to kill me. I want you to try it this morning! You will see that I can whip you for the ninth time!"

Pedro cringed. *What can I do? Roberto is so drunk it would be easy to beat him up. But beating up a drunken man isn't looked upon too kindly in Kusulí. Besides, I don't want to beat him up. I want to kill him.*

Pedro stepped back into the house so Roberto wouldn't see him. Maybe he would just pass on by and leave him in peace. But Roberto staggered right up to the house and continued to rant.

"So you're jealous about your wife, eh? You think I love her. And now you want to kill me. Come on out! Let's fight it out right here! Let's see who kills who!"

Pedro slipped out the back door and hid behind the house. Roberto staggered into the house, searching for him. When he didn't find him, he howled, "He's scared of me! That's what he is. That chicken ran off!"

Pedro was in an awful rage. He stalked back into the banana grove to get his anger under control. He saw Roberto staggering down the road again, on his way to the saloon. Pedro decided to return home, so he crossed the road and entered his house. Unfortunately, Roberto saw him. He swung around and headed back to confront his enemy in his own home.

Pedro shut the front door. But Roberto was desperate. He kicked the door open. "You beast! Why are you scared of me? I've whipped you eight times, and today will be the ninth. You say you're going to kill me. So kill me if you want. You claim I am in love with your wife. Well, it's true. What are you going to do about it?"

When Pedro heard these last words, the devil entered his heart and filled him with uncontrollable rage. He slipped into his bedroom to find a weapon. He knew Roberto expected to fight with bare hands. But he wanted a machete.

The only machete in the bedroom was short, dull, and work-worn. "It will have to do," he hissed under his breath.

He met Roberto in the living room. "There you are, you rascal!" Roberto yelled. "Are you ready?"

Roberto took several steps toward him. Pedro sidestepped and slashed at Roberto's leg with the machete. It caught him right below the knee and drew blood. Roberto howled in pain and bent over, grabbing his wounded knee with both hands. This was Pedro's chance.

Pedro raised his machete high and brought it down with all his might onto the back of Roberto's neck. Roberto fell like an ox, blood spurting from the wound. Pedro stared in horror at what he had done. Fear and rage engulfed his heart. As a man possessed, he whacked away at Roberto's neck.

When only a piece of skin still held Roberto's head to his body, Pedro stopped whacking. He grabbed Roberto's head by the hair and sawed through the skin. Then, still carrying his machete, he ran outside and threw the head onto the road. Seeing a bunch of neighbors gathering around, Pedro did the only thing he could think to do. He ran. The last thing the Kusulí people saw of Pedro was a desperate young man, carrying a machete still dripping with blood, running over the crest of the hill behind his house.

The sun was still above the western horizon when they found Don Pancho. He was at his church house enjoying an afternoon service. As he traveled toward Kusulí, he felt a terrible sadness, but he was not surprised. It was the end he had expected.

Approximately two hundred people were gathered on the road around Roberto's head when Don Pancho arrived at the scene. Don Pancho stood and stared at his son's head. It had shriveled in death. It did not look like his son at all. Because all the blood had drained from the vessels, the head seemed a third smaller than usual. On impulse, Don Pancho reached down and picked it up by the ear. His voice broke as he lifted the head high for all to see and began slowly, "Roberto, Roberto, it's been a long time since I have had the privilege of pulling your ear. I never dreamed I would do it like this. Son, this is what had to happen to you because of your rebellion."

Then, turning to face the crowd, Don Pancho continued. "This is what happens to a young man who doesn't obey his parents or respect the Lord God Almighty. Listen, young people, here is a lesson to be learned. If you blaspheme God, this will be your cost." Then he dropped the head into a sack and went to see the body.

On his way to Kusulí, Don Pancho had stopped at Tim Schrock's place and asked him to come in his jeep to help move the body. Tim promised to come down after his chores. Tim arrived while it was still daylight, but the police had not arrived yet. Until they came, no one could touch the body. The police didn't arrive until several hours later. By the time Tim and Don Pancho had loaded the body and the head, it was late.

They bumped along for almost an hour until they arrived at the chapel where Don Pancho worshiped. It was nine o'clock. His pastor, Don Tirso, and a multitude of friends and neighbors were there to receive them.

By the time Don Pancho entered the church building, they had set up a table for the body. People made way as they carried the body in and laid it on the table. The bloody stump was more than a lot of people could stomach. But, in war-torn Nicaragua, the sight was not so unusual.

Roberto's mother wept as she stared at her son's headless body. One of Roberto's sisters wailed, "This is from the hand of the Lord! This is from the hand of the Lord!" Everyone knew it was true.

Then Don Pancho walked out into the darkness and brought in the sack. People made way for him as he approached the head of the makeshift table. He reached deep into the sack. He got his son's head by both ears this time and held it high. Then he cleared his throat. Everyone was quiet. Too quiet.

"Listen, my friends. This is what happens when a young man defies God. Many people have tried to tell Roberto that he should change his ways. He never listened. Yesterday, he and his brother, Alfredo, met me in the cacao patch. For the last time, I tried to reason with him. I told him about a dream I had where he was killed. But as usual, all he could do was laugh. Listen, my friends! If we mock God and reject Him, this is what happens. This is a lesson for us all!

"Yes, I am sad that my son died. Especially in this way, and living in sin. And yet, I am not surprised. I know this is from the hand of the Lord God Almighty, so why should I be opposed?"

Don Pancho lowered his son's head and put it at its place, the severed head against the mangled stump. Then they covered him with a sheet.

It was pitch dark outside the church house. The darkness invaded every corner of the chapel. Many people walked up to the table and stared at Roberto's shriveled face. Handsome in life, in death he wore the ghastly look of the doomed. People shook their heads sadly. Everyone knew he had received his dues. Everyone agreed with his sister's verdict. This was from the hand of the Lord.

————————————

We can imagine Roberto writhing in pain, the sulfur and smoke choking him. Finding no relief, his thoughts only added to his torment. There was no rest from his awful thoughts!

Roberto's thoughts were as crystal clear as when he was still alive on earth. If anything, they seemed clearer, because in this place the only distraction was constant pain. He could think only truth here. The truth was killing him, yet he could never die! *Why, oh, why did I never face reality on earth? Why did I ignore the fact that God had created me and thus owned me? I was totally His, and yet I chose to serve His enemy.*

Oh, if only I would have done what my dad and mom used to tell me! If only I would have listened to my dad and Pablo and the many others who talked to me about my soul!

Roberto gnashed his teeth in pain. *Please!* he screamed. *Someone send a drop of water! Please, tell Alfredo what it's like down here so he can straighten up his life! Please, tell Pedro to repent! Tell my dad that he was right after all! Warn my two little boys so they won't follow my example!*

Chapter Four

THE PRICE PAID IN FULL

Bright stars twinkled like tiny, shiny eyes watching the drama about to unfold on that dark Kusulí night. The date was May 2, 1997.[11] The hour was 10 p.m. Twenty-four-year-old Fausto Sánchez already considered himself a seasoned robber. This fearless spokesman in countless robberies, assaults, and kidnappings now crouched behind the *rancho* like a fugitive. Something was definitely wrong. Tonight he was afraid.

Swallowing thick saliva, he took another step toward the two-story wooden house that loomed above him not more than thirty feet from the *rancho*. He shook his head bewilderedly. *Why am I such a chicken tonight?*

Fausto looked up into the sky. He saw the twinkling stars. They seemed brighter to him than he had ever seen them before. Then he thought of God, and in his heart he knew exactly what was causing him to be a wimp that night—it was the words the lead robber, Ronald Artola, had spoken only minutes before when they were ready to assault the *gringos'* house. Hiding in the shadows of the clump of banana trees, Ronald had whispered, "Look, tonight we are going to get dollars

---

11 *Read the missionaries' side of the story in* Angels in the Night, *chapter five.*

from these *gringos*. Lots of dollars. But I don't want any of you guys to lift a finger to hurt them. They are godly people. Don't you dare touch a hair on their heads!"

Fausto noticed that his hands were trembling. Fear clutched at his heart like it never had before during any of his many other robberies. Not even the first time he took part in a robbery, when he was a teenager and his brother Jorge was teaching him to steal.

Fausto gripped his machine gun tightly, forcing his hands to become solid like steel, as they usually were during a robbery. He swallowed again. Then he took another step—a step that took him out from behind the *rancho* and exposed him to the open night. He shook his head again. *I can't do it,* he muttered. He stepped back into the shadow of the *rancho,* then stalked back to the opposite end where his buddy, Paco Artola, was waiting.

"Paco, I can't do it," Fausto whispered hoarsely. "Ronald said they are godly people. How can we know that God won't deal with us tonight? I respect Christian people, don't you?"

This was the first time that Paco, Ronald's younger brother, was helping with an outright assault. The light-skinned, short, stocky man was already afraid. He nodded and whispered back. "I know they are good people."

"I am going to talk to Ronald," Fausto ventured. He walked back down over the sloping yard to the banana patch and met Ronald and Fausto's cousin, Ezequiel, in the dim starlight.

"What's wrong?" Ronald hissed.

"Look," Fausto grunted, "I don't think we should steal from these people. You said yourself that they are good people. God could deal with us tonight. Those guys could shoot us. You know how prepared *gringos* are. They might be well-armed. I can't make myself holler at them."

"Man, what happened to you, chicken?" Ronald mocked. "Where's big, tough Fausto? I've never seen you like this before. There is absolutely nothing to be afraid of. These people are harmless and don't even own guns. You are a big fat chicken, that's what you are!"

"You tell me they are nice, so why would we want to hurt them?"

"We are not going to hurt them. I made that clear. They have easy dollars. That's why we are here. We're not backing out, now that we're this close."

"Why don't you go then, if you think it's so easy?"

"You know I can't go. Those guys know me too well. I talk with them almost every Wednesday. They rent my house in Waslala for their services, and I often go visit with them before church to practice my English. They would recognize my voice immediately. Cut out that mystic fear and get the gut back," Ronald swore. Fausto turned and trudged up the slope toward the house. Though he was still afraid and knew he would hate himself for doing it, he couldn't back out now. There were few things harder to face than Ronald Artola's scorn.

Paco clung to the shadows. Fausto stepped out into the open the second time, gripping his machine gun as if his life depended on it. *Why am I afraid?* he asked himself again. He took a deep breath and then looked up into the sky and wondered if there was still a way he could stop this robbery. The huge fear gripped him again, as if his whole chest were held tightly in a vise, and suddenly it was hard to breath. He felt sure that God was warning him. His voice sounded hoarse as he forced his vocal cords to shout, *"Don Pablo, ábranos!* (Mr. Pablo, open up!)"

A German shepherd scampered out from the porch, barking madly. Fausto stepped behind a tree, but stood his ground. He wasn't afraid of dogs. The dog circled him, barking viciously, but Fausto totally ignored him. He watched the house like an owl. Then he hollered again, *"Don Pablo, ábranos!"*

A wooden shutter from the top story was thrown open. The window looked dark, and Fausto could barely see a form in it. Then the man in the window shone the beam of a flashlight right into his face. Fausto knew the tricks to the trade. As soon as the light was on him, he picked up the machine gun, exposing it clearly, yet protecting his body behind the tree. *If they are armed, they will shoot now,* Fausto knew.

But there was only silence, except for the growling of the mutt that still circled him. Then, to Fausto's surprise, a man's voice rang out into the darkness. The voice was not angry. There was no panic. Only a controlled, calm, "What can I do for you, sirs?"

"Come on down. We need to talk to you," Fausto answered. "Don't be afraid."

There was a long pause. Then the man at the window answered, "I'll be right down. Just give me time to get dressed."

Paco had crept over to the edge of the *rancho* and was listening to the conversation. *This man should be no problem,* he decided. His voice actually sounded friendly. Honest. Straightforward.

Since this was Paco's first armed robbery, he felt not only afraid, but very vulnerable. Yes, he carried one of Ronald's three machine guns, but he knew he was not nearly as prepared as the other three robbers who had not only carried the death machines, but had used them. Fausto himself had told him what all was involved in being a big-time robber and kidnapper. Though Paco had decided to give it a try, he really wondered if he could shoot if he had to. *What have I gotten myself into?* Paco argued with himself. *This is crazy!*

Minutes later, the downstairs door opened and Fausto could see the silhouette of a man as he walked toward them, hissing at the dog, trying to make her shut up.

"Over here," Fausto called out quietly.

Pablo walked right up to them. "We are the Recontra," Fausto lied, cradling his machine gun in his arms. "We want you to cooperate with us. We want some food." *We'll start slowly,* Fausto decided. *I can talk about food so they really think we are the Recontra. And the food thing kind of breaks the ice.*

"Sure. What would you like? I have bread and cheese. I can make you some coffee."

"Do you have tortillas?"

"I am sorry; my wife doesn't make tortillas, but we have plenty of bread. How many of you are there?"

"There are eight of us," Fausto lied again. "We'll take the bread and cheese."

After Pablo disappeared back into the house, Paco grinned. "This is going to be easy. That guy is very cooperative." But Fausto was silent.

The next thing the two robbers knew, Pablo was back, carrying a tray full of chunks of white cheese and plenty of bread. "I've got the coffee pot on," he said kindly.

"No, no, we can't eat here," Fausto stammered. "Find a bag and we will carry it with us."

Before Pablo returned to the house, Fausto threw in quickly, "We need 5,000 córdobas ($600) tonight."

"I am sorry," Pablo answered sincerely. "We don't have that kind of money. I have a little bit on me, but since the robbers hit us often, we just don't keep much money on hand."

"Go get what you've got!" Fausto barked.

Pablo disappeared again.

"I bet they're lying," Paco whispered. "I bet they have all kinds of money."

Fausto was quiet, thinking hard.

When Pablo came back, the money in his hand, Fausto commanded, "Count it."

Pablo counted out 120 córdobas. That was all.

"Who else is here with you?" Fausto asked.

"Just the schoolteacher. He stays here with us."

"Go get the schoolteacher's money."

"I'm afraid he won't have any, but I will go get him."

The two robbers followed Pablo over to the front door. Inside, a single light bulb shone brightly. Outside on the porch, they felt protected by the darkness. Fausto's fear had mostly left him now, but for some reason he still felt sad. *Sure enough,* he mused, *these people are nice and easy to work with. It really is stupid to be stealing from them, though.*

Pablo returned with the schoolteacher. Standing in the doorway, tall and fearless, the teacher said, "Good evening. How are you all doing?"

"Good evening," Fausto returned. "We want your money. All of it."

"I am sorry," the young man answered. "I don't have any money. The last time the robbers came, they took the last 200 córdobas I had."

"Come on," Paco pitched in sternly. "You've got money. Go get it."

"Listen," Pablo broke in, "we have been robbed thirteen times. Tonight, it is fourteen times. Do you think it is wise for us to have money on us? But if you don't believe us, you may search the house."

Paco punched Fausto secretly and then disappeared down to the garden where Ronald and Ezequiel were hiding. Minutes later, he was back. Breathlessly he said, "The top guy says there has to be money. If not, we are going to take one of you guys to the jungle. He means business."

"Wait," Fausto snapped at Paco. "Don't start with that yet." Then, turning to Pablo, he continued. "We are going to the other gringo's house to get his money. Let's go. Both of you."

"Please, sir," Pablo asked, concern in his voice, "could this fellow stay? I don't like to leave my family alone."

"That's fine," Fausto answered. "He can stay."

The schoolteacher went back into the house. Fausto told Pablo to stay put, then he and Paco sprinted down to the garden. "What is taking so long?" Ronald whispered angrily.

"They don't have much money at all."

"What do you mean they don't have money? Of course they do. *Gringos* always use a lot of money. I lived in Wisconsin for several years, and I know how they operate."

"Well, these guys say they've been robbed fourteen times," Fausto muttered defensively. "They made it clear that they never keep money on hand."

"That's a lie," Ronald sassed. "We are getting dollars tonight—"

"Wait," Fausto broke in. "Right now we are going to the other fellow's house to get what he has."

As Fausto turned to go, Ronald hissed, "How much did you get from Don Pablo?"

"I'll tell you later," Fausto answered.

As Fausto and Paco headed back to the house, Ronald swore and fumed. "Those *gringos* have money," Ronald said angrily. "They are just outwitting Fausto, that's all. Or Fausto is outwitting us!"

Ezequiel nodded.

Back at the house, Fausto commanded Pablo, "Let's go to your friend's house. You go ahead."

As they walked down the hill past the garden where Ronald was hiding, Fausto was surprised when Pablo hollered out, *"Buenas noches"* to his buddies in hiding. What surprised him more was that Ronald answered in a low, clear grunt! Carelessly, Fausto flashed his light over toward the clump of bananas.

Pablo walked ahead, and Fausto followed him. Paco came last in line as they crossed Tim's foot bridge and hiked up the other side of the gully. Fausto was surprised at how calm Pablo seemed. He could almost detect joy in his step! *I wonder why he isn't afraid,* Fausto thought.

When they arrived at the other *gringo's* house, Pablo called until Tim finally woke up. He came out onto the little balcony on the second story and looked down at them. Fausto saw that he was a tall, skinny man. Pablo quickly told him, "Some *amigos* here need money. They say you should bring it all."

Tim disappeared into the house and soon was back with a wad of money. "I do have some money today," he announced. "I usually don't have this much, but I brought it from Waslala to pay for a tree that I bought to cut up for timber for our new church house. It's about 350 córdobas ($45)." Then he leaned over and dropped the money into Pablo's hands. Pablo counted it and gave it to the robber. Fausto stuck the money in his pocket.

"Come on down, Tim. We need to talk to you," Fausto barked.

Tim came down quickly and met the robber at the front door. "Hey," Fausto snapped, "you have more money than this. Out with it. You guys have to have money to operate your farms."

Carefully and calmly, Tim explained, "Look, we have had many robberies, and we can't keep money on us here. That would make the robbers come more than ever. We keep our money in Waslala. We don't lie because we are Christians. But, if you like, you may search my house."

Fausto knew what the tall *gringo* was telling him was true. He also knew that he would have a terrible time convincing Ronald. *I had better search the house,* Fausto concluded. *If not, how will I make Ronald happy?*

"I'll search the house," Fausto said.

"May I bring my wife out? She's pretty frightened," Tim told the robber.

"Sure."

Minutes later, Rosa stepped out onto the dark porch. Fausto and Paco were both surprised that she wasn't more afraid. Usually the women got hysterical during robberies. Rosa looked frightened, but collected. In the starlight, she looked different than any woman they had ever seen. She wore a long dress and a white cloth on her head. Fausto shook his head again. *What are we doing here, stealing from these people?*

In front of the house was a board plopped down on two blocks of wood. Fausto motioned the *gringos* to sit down on the makeshift bench. Then he whispered to Paco, "Keep an eye on them. I'm going to search the house."

Paco stood out in the yard in the dark in front of the three *gringos*. He gripped his machine gun, and the trigger felt cold to his touch. *I hope Fausto hurries,* he thought. Across the valley behind the house Paco heard some dogs barking. *I bet there's a house over there. I hope they don't find out what's going on.* He shivered.

The moon was only a sliver, but the stars were very bright. In the starlight he could see the dark forms of the three *gringos*. The tall one called Tim sat there, shirtless and barefooted, his wife beside him with that white cloth on her head, and the preacher, whom everyone called Pablo, sat beside her. Paco reached up and pulled his beret down lower over his face, though the *gringos* didn't know him, so he was in no danger of being recognized.

Paco was disappointed. So far they had been able to get very little money. They claimed that they never kept any money on them. Paco suspected that it was true. Many tales came through the grapevine of the many robbers who had visited the *gringos*. No, they usually didn't find much money, it was said, but there were always things to take, and the *gringos* were nice to all the robbers who came.

Meanwhile, Fausto was searching for money. He went upstairs right away, guessing they would keep the money in their bedroom. He checked their dresser and found no money. A nice, compact Bible on the dresser caught his attention. *I used to be a Christian,* he mused. *A long time ago. I used to have a Bible. I bet these people read their Bible a lot.* Absentmindedly, he picked up the Bible and looked it over. He opened and closed the zipper. *I wish I had a Bible like this,* he thought. *But I respect it too much to steal it.* He replaced it reverently.

Fausto picked up the mat on the bed. Nothing.

As Paco guarded the three hostages on the bench, he sensed they weren't afraid. That was strange. Suddenly, Paco heard soft humming from the lady with the white cloth on her head. Then the preacher began to sing along with her. Quietly at first, then Tim joined in, and the song got louder. Paco's heart was warmed. The music was lovely. These people really knew how to sing! Then something more than the music struck him. It was the words: "Cover me; fill my life with Your consolation; keep me; keep my life during the storm."

The next song was meaningful, too: "A wonderful Saviour is Jesus my Lord, a wonderful Saviour to me. . . ."

Fausto heard the singing, too. He marveled as he continued to ransack the house. The same question that haunted Paco bothered him. *How can these people sing when they are being accosted by robbers?*

What in the world makes these people sing? Paco wondered. *How can they sing when I stand here in front of them with an AK machine gun, watching their every move? How can they praise God when my armed buddy tears up their house? This can't be true. Am I dreaming?*

Then the trio started to sing another song. "Then sings my soul, my Saviour God, to Thee: How great Thou art! How great Thou art!"

Maybe that's why they aren't afraid, Paco concluded. *They trust in that great God they sing about. But how can they trust Him if He allows them to be robbed again and again?*

Paco felt sad as he listened to them sing. Until recently, he had been a Christian in a local Evangelical church. Now he had fallen away. *I wish I could still be faithful to God,* Paco sighed to himself. *I wish I could feel what they feel. I know they love God. I can sense it clearly. Even if we come to steal their things, they are still full of joy. I need to get my heart right with God again. Why am I out here stealing? I am selling my soul to Satan.* Tears welled up in Paco's eyes, and his heart was touched deeply.

After a bit, Pablo asked quietly, "May I pray?" Paco couldn't answer.

Pablo took his silence for a yes and started to pray out loud in clear Spanish. Paco's mouth turned dry and he licked his lips. The man was thanking God for the robbery! He was pleading for his wife and his children. He was asking for God's protection over the three who sat there on the bench. It sounded just as if Pablo was talking to somebody right there with them. Maybe that Somebody *was* there!

Paco's heart thumped loudly in his chest. He tried his best to hide his emotions. Pablo was praying for him now. In sincere tones, he thanked his Lord for the opportunity to meet with his new *amigos*, and Paco knew he referred to them, the robbers.

Tears slipped down Paco's cheeks. Pablo was praying for his salvation. It felt as if something or someone had his heart clutched in a fist. His breathing was heavy, and he began to sweat as he heard the pleading tones. "Father, I pray for this man in front of us. Please touch his heart with Your love. You know we love him, Father. Help him feel Your love through us.

Help him choose to serve You. Help him repent from his sins and seek Your face . . ."

Fausto heard the praying, too. He was downstairs now, going through the kitchen cabinets. But he wasn't finding any money. When Pablo started to pray, he stopped and listened. It struck his heart and helped to make this the most difficult robbery he had ever participated in.

Paco could hardly stand the pleading tones. Thought after thought tumbled into his heart and made him tremble all over. *What if I would fling my gun aside and run over to them and kneel down and tell them that I want to repent? I could tell them that I want to have the peace and joy they have. I know they would accept me and pray for me. I could leave this life of sin and be free. Oh, how I long for a life like theirs!*

But what would Fausto say? Worse yet, what would my brother Ronald say? He would mock me to no end. He would never forgive me. I would have to confess everything to these people, and it would get the whole gang in trouble. They might even kill me. I just can't do it. The prayer ended. Paco's decision was made, and he hissed at Fausto. The neighbor's dogs were barking furiously and they might soon be found out. "Hurry!" he hissed again.

Finally, Fausto stepped out of the house, carrying his machine gun and a tote bag full of things he had collected. He approached the three hostages.

"May I have a black zipper Bible I saw upstairs?" Fausto asked.

"Ask my wife," Tim answered kindly. "It's hers."

"May I have your Bible?" Fausto asked Rosa.

"Well, yes . . ." Rosa answered hesitantly.

"Look, if you give it to me voluntarily, I will take it. If not, just say so and I won't touch it."

"Well," Rosa answered, "I would appreciate if you would let me take my things out of it first. Then you can have it gladly."

Fausto sprinted up the stairs and soon returned, handing Rosa her Bible. Rosa opened the zipper carefully and took out all of her precious things—letters of encouragement and photos. Then she handed the Bible back to Fausto with a smile. "You can take it gladly," Rosa announced.

Tim laid his hand on Fausto's shoulder and said in that same quiet, steady voice, "*Amigo,* I want you to read this book. Read what it says and put it to practice. It can bring salvation to your life. You need to repent from your wicked ways."

"I have never been a Christian," Fausto lied. "Maybe someday I'll become one."

"That's good," Tim added. "Remember, God loves you."

As Tim pled with the robber, Paco was troubled again. He knew that what he was saying was not only true for his friend. It was true for him too. *I know I should repent. I should seek God and change my ways. I don't want to go to hell. I would love to go to heaven like these people . . .*

Someday I will do it, but not tonight.

Suddenly, Fausto was all business again. The neighbor's dogs were barking louder than ever. "We'll go over to Pablo's house to talk to the boss. He will not be happy that there is still no money."

"Is it all right if Tim and his wife come with us?" Pablo asked cautiously. "They won't be able to sleep anyway."

"Sure," Fausto snapped. "Hurry! March!"

The three hostages walked ahead of the robbers in the dark. Fausto followed, carrying the AK machine gun. He was worried. He knew there was trouble ahead. *I need to get rougher with these people so we can get some money out of them, or Ronald will be furious. But I can't make myself be mean to these people.*

Paco came last in the train, keenly aware of the big gun he carried. The stars twinkled like a trillion bright eyes. God seemed close. *This is all wrong. I should not be here doing this. God is speaking to me.*

The dog barked furiously again as the robbers approached Pablo's house. Ronald had disappeared. It was obvious that he was afraid. The whole deal was taking way too long. Fausto was nervous, not knowing what to do next. But the ordeal was still far from over.

"May Rosa go inside to be with the others?" Tim asked.

"No. We are not done yet," Fausto answered. Then he left to find Ronald. Paco stayed guarding the trio. Fausto found Ronald and Ezequiel down over the hill, hiding in a gully.

Ronald was furious. "You idiot," he snarled. "When you came past earlier, you shone at us with your flashlight. Where are your brains? I had to throw myself flat on the dirt so those *gringos* wouldn't see me."

Fausto was quiet, but anger was growing in his chest.

Ronald kept insisting that there had to be money and hissed at Fausto, "Tell those guys that there has to be money or we will kidnap one of them."

As Fausto approached the house, fear struck him again. *What if these men shoot us?* Though he was convinced that they were harmless, he needed to be sure. Walking up to the hostages, he made a decision.

"Raise your arms," he barked.

Pablo and Tim obediently raised their arms. Fausto frisked them carefully, but he found no guns. Then he motioned to the two men to follow him. He led them to a guayaba tree on a knoll beside the house. Paco stayed close to Rosa.

The air was tense now. The time had come to stop playing games. "Look," he commanded, "the boss says that there has to be money. Either you come up with 5,000 córdobas ($600) now, or we take Tim to the jungle and you, Pablo, get twenty thousand córdobas ($2500.00) together by tomorrow at ten o'clock."

Fausto was surprised when Pablo's answer was delivered with a determined calm. "I want to talk with the boss."

"Nope, he would never allow that," Fausto said.

"I want to explain why we can't give ransom money for kidnapping," Pablo pled. "I want to tell him personally."

"This isn't a kidnapping," Fausto snapped.

"It sure looks like that's what you are suggesting," Pablo answered gently.

"The boss won't come up here, but I will tell him what you say. Just tell me."

Pablo took a deep breath and plunged into his explanation. "Our mission has decided that we won't give ransom money for kidnappings. If we did, you know we would be sunk. You would be back. Other robbers would hit us. Eventually our mission would have to close down. We would have to leave, and what would happen with our little church? There would be no more preaching and no more clinic. We can't let that happen. We love our mission too much for that. That's why we can't give you ransom money."

Tall and fearless, Tim broke in. "That's right. We'd rather give our lives than let this mission die. But if you insist on taking me, I am ready anytime."

Pablo was leaning against the guayaba tree trunk, his right hand clutching a branch above him. *I wonder if he is afraid,* Fausto pondered. *He probably is. Yet he doesn't realize that in other robberies we would beat a man to a pulp for stalling like he is. He doesn't know that many men have been shot for such words. But for some reason I know they aren't bluffing. They mean what they say. What in the world will I tell Ronald?*

Pablo spoke again. "Yes, you can take either of us. We are ready. But if you plan to shoot us later when there is no ransom money, you may just as well get it over with and do it here and now."

Fausto was floored. He had never heard anything like it. Fausto felt all his evil power against them drain out of his system. The devil lost his grip on his man. *I can't keep on doing this,* Fausto muttered. Then he shivered, and the fear returned.

"Could you just please just get me 2,000 córdobas ($250)?" Fausto's voice had lost all of its snap. *That would at least make Ronald happier.*

"I am sorry," Pablo answered. "If we had it, we would have gladly given it to you already. We don't have any more money."

"Just get me 1,000 then," Fausto begged.

"Listen, I will explain one more time," Pablo said patiently. "We are Christians and don't lie. We don't have any more money. But if you want to search the house, you may. Or you may take anything you find."

Postponing his confrontation with Ronald, Fausto decided on the spot, "I will search the house." *Maybe Ronald will believe me that way.*

"Could you do the search carefully?" Pablo ventured. "My family has been scarred by all these robberies, and they are afraid tonight."

"Tell them all to come down," Fausto demanded.

Pablo protested. "We have a bunch of neighbor girls here who are sleeping with my girls. I would sure hate for them to have to wake up to this ordeal."

"Get them down," Fausto barked.

Pablo disappeared into the dark house. Fausto felt badly that he had forced them to come down. After seeing how long it was taking Pablo to get the people up, he hissed to Tim, "Just tell them to stay in one of the bedrooms."

Tim caught the group as they were coming down the stairs. The family and the girls quickly returned to their room, and Pablo and Tim returned to face their *amigos*. This time, Fausto positioned them in the carport and asked Paco to watch them again. Calling Pablo into the house, he asked, "Do you people have guns?"

Pablo hesitated. Then he said slowly, "No, we don't own guns. We are Christians. But my son has a BB gun, and it looks an awful lot like a twenty-two. I think I'd better tell you about it now, rather than for you to find it later and get mad at me for lying."

Man, this guy is honest, Fausto concluded. "Bring it," he demanded. Pablo brought the BB gun. *I won't take that thing,* Fausto decided. *That's just a toy, and I have a real machine gun.* "Let it go," he said. Pablo laid it aside.

Then Fausto sent Pablo out and searched the house. Just like Fausto expected, he found no money. But when he searched the girls' room, he remembered his girlfriend. He started to add things to his bag that she would like. He took several perfumes, a pair of nice shoes, and other pretty things that girls like. Fifteen minutes later, he realized that Ronald would be furious. *I've got to get out of here,* Fausto decided.

Fausto met Tim, Rosa, and Pablo in the carport. The first thing he said was, "Look, don't you dare get us in trouble. Don't call on the radio tonight or let the police know. If you do, remember, we know where you live, and we will come get you!"

"Thanks for not being rough with us tonight," Pablo stammered.

"Thanks for being nice and for opening up right away," Fausto answered. "What really makes us angry is when people don't open up."

Paco shook his head in the dark. *They are saying thankyou to each other like old friends!*

The school teacher had made coffee almost two hours earlier. He joined them in the carport. Pablo handed the thermos to Fausto and whispered, "It's for you." Rosa had remembered to bring along a freshly baked cake which she insisted that the robbers take. Then Pablo searched for the bread and cheese he had packed earlier and left in the carport.

"The dogs hauled off the bread and cheese," Pablo announced, chuckling. "Too bad."

Fausto was standing out in the yard now, obviously ready to leave. Quietly he said, "Goodnight," then turned on his heel and left. The *gringos* all returned his goodnight.

Paco felt a strange impulse to do more. He stepped back into the carport, switching his machine gun to his left hand. He shook hands with Pablo first. "Goodnight," he said gently.

Pablo answered, "May God bless you!"

Then he shook hands with Tim and Rosa and the schoolteacher, and they all gave him their blessing. The *gringos* quickly went inside and closed the door.

The two robbers marched down the hill to face the boss. Just as they expected, he was very angry.

"Did you get the big money?" Ronald growled right away.

"No, we didn't," Fausto answered, at a loss for what to say next. "They didn't have any. I searched both houses well."

"Why didn't you bring Tim?" Ronald complained. "We could have given him a real scare and acted as if we were hauling him off. If we would have at least hauled him to the woods, Pablo would have gotten the money around. I am sure he would've."

Fausto shrugged. "I just couldn't do it. Like you said, they are way too nice. Plus, their mission has a policy that they don't give ransom money."

"Man, you are a wimp! I didn't want you to hurt them, but you could have pressured them a lot more and brought one along to take to the jungle. You are a chicken!"

The anger in Fausto's chest was growing fast. He had just come through one of the roughest robberies in his life. He knew he hadn't done a good job as a robber, which frustrated him. But maybe, in the long run, he'd done what was best. By far, the worst part of the whole evening was hearing Ronald spew out his venom. He hadn't even lifted a finger in the robbery! Fausto could feel the hair on his neck rise at Ronald's unreasonable accusations. The evening suddenly turned explosive as the two men faced each other in the dark.

"How much money did you get?" Ronald asked. His voice was as cold as ice.

"Not much," Fausto answered lamely, "Maybe 500 córdobas ($65)." Fausto reached into his pocket to pull out the cash.

"What do you have in your tote bag?" Ronald demanded.

"Just little knickknacks for my girlfriend."

Suddenly Ronald lost his head. Taking a quick step toward Fausto, he raised his machine gun level with his chest and cursed. Then he snarled, "Hand over the money, you snake in the weeds! You are a big fat liar. You have collected at least 10,000 córdobas ($1250) tonight. You aren't going to pull the wool over my eyes, you rascal!"

Nobody moved. Paco stood beside Fausto and Ezequiel stood behind Ronald. All three knew this was a showdown. Ronald and Fausto were not used to stepping down to anybody. But Ronald didn't realize what all Fausto had been through during this difficult robbery, or how frustrated and angry he was.

What made Fausto most angry was the fact that Ronald had accused him of treason. Robbers always divided the loot fairly. If a robber hogged the loot, he was stealing twice—once from the victim, and again from his buddies. That was anathema. The accusation lit the wick of Fausto's fury.

Fausto exploded. He didn't have to do much to bring Ronald to his knees. Fausto's gun was ready. It always was. In a fraction of a second, he jerked it to position and pulled the trigger. The shot ripped apart the already tense night.

Fausto's shot was well-calculated. He wasn't planning to kill Ronald. He didn't even want to hurt him. But he did want to scare him and show him that he meant business. The bullet ripped open the red clay right at Ronald's feet. Ronald leaped back in terror, almost falling over. Fausto also jumped—right up to Ronald. Now, as Ronald opened his eyes, he was looking right up the barrel of Fausto's machine gun. Fausto was taller than Ronald by a full eight inches, and he stared down at his target in the starlight. Fausto's arms were as hard as steel again, and the tough devil in him had returned full force.

Ronald was trembling all over as he stuttered, "What do you mean, man? I wasn't going to hurt you. I just want you to divide up the loot fairly."

Suddenly, Fausto was trembling all over too. He realized how easy it would have been for him to kill Ronald. "You coward!" Fausto spit between his teeth. "Don't you ever dare accuse me of treason again! All I got was 500 córdobas, and if you want the measly catch, here it is."

Before Fausto could pull the money out of his pocket, Ronald and Ezequiel swung around and fled. After they had disappeared into the shadows, Fausto turned to Paco, still shaking, and chuckled, "Boy that was close!"

"It served that bully right," Paco answered.

Fausto and Paco slowly retraced their path to Waslala that night. They didn't want to catch up with Ronald and Ezequiel. As they walked, they talked. Fausto, the talkative one, was quiet and subdued. But Paco's tongue was loosened by the excitement of the evening. "My brother is crazy," he muttered. "Since he can't be involved in the robbery, he can't accept it when things don't turn out his way."

"I felt like shooting him," Fausto admitted. "He made me so mad!"

For a long time they talked about the strange people they had spent the evening with. "Aren't those people different?" Paco asked. "A person can't help but be nice to them. You'll never find a Nicaraguan that will be as cooperative and nice as they are."

"And I can't help but believe that they tell the truth," Fausto added. "It makes me feel horrible to steal from them."

"Exactly! I will never steal from those people again. When they started singing, it really got to me," Paco confessed. "Just a month ago I was still going to church and trying to be a Christian. I know I am being awfully wicked stealing like this."

Fausto sneered, "Maybe you should recommit your life to God."

"Well, you don't know how those songs made me feel. They actually made me cry . . . especially that song *How Great Thou Art*. I felt as if something was clutching my heart. I actually thought about what it would be like to go to them and ask them to pray for me. But I knew I couldn't, because Ronald is such a rat!"

"Did you see that I got a Bible from them?"

"Yes, I heard it all. Maybe you will become a Christian too, someday. I would really like to. I'm sure it would be better than going on stealing like this."

When they got to Waslala, the two young men parted ways, each with his own thoughts to sort out. Fausto never dreamed that he would never see his bosom friend again. Neither of them had any way of knowing what lay just around the corner, and it was just as well they didn't.

The day after the robbery, Fausto hunted up his new enemy. Ronald's house was perched high up on a bank right off the road that crossed Papayo Hill. Fausto strode up the road, then jogged up the steep trail toward his house. He could see that Ronald had just gotten out of bed and was having a cup of coffee, lying in his hammock which hung in the small open porch. He looked as if he'd had roofing nails for breakfast.

"*Buenas*, (Hello)" Fausto said as he strode across the yard.

"*Buenas*," Ronald grunted, sitting up in his hammock. "What do you want now?"

"I came to give you the money we made on our operation last night," Fausto said as he pulled the small wad out of his pocket. "I never did want to do that robbery, but you insisted. I knew it was a mistake. And, to tell you the truth, I don't want a stitch of this stinking money. If I could, I would give it back to those people." Fausto threw the wad onto Ronald's lap.

Ronald's eyes were half closed. He had a wicked grin on his face as he spit between his teeth. "I never knew the great Fausto Sánchez could be such a sissy. And I never expected that he would turn on me, either."

But Fausto was already crossing the yard, leaving as fast as he could. When he heard Ronald's last comment, he turned around just long enough to fling out his last words. "Don't ever expect me to go with you on another job!"

"Don't worry, I won't need you." Ronald's words echoed in Fausto's heart as he bounded down the steep bank toward the road.

Waslala was in an uproar. A well-armed, well-masked robber band had stopped a European Union's project vehicle several miles out of Waslala. They'd been driving in from Managua. Everyone was sure that the robbers were after the German who ran the project. But he happened not to be along that day, so they whisked off the next highest in command, a dark-skinned Nicaraguan called Armando.

Ronald Artola was the kidnapper. He badly needed the money, and he had come up with a big plan which he was sure would succeed. He was certain he would get the money to head back to the U.S., but he needed help getting it.

Fausto's brothers, Jorge and Vicente, also big-time robbers, had left the area. Since Ronald was not about to ask Fausto, he asked his cousin Ezequiel to go along with him again, and he asked Paco to join them. This would be Paco's second robbery, and it would be a big one, including a kidnapping. Ronald also hired a man who worked with the European Union as a guard at their Waslala offices to cooperate with information.

The plan seemed fail-proof, but Ronald was disgusted when he discovered that the German wasn't in the vehicle. Making the best of the situation, he hauled Armando to the jungle and sent word to the Europeans that he wanted a huge sum of money.

The Europeans didn't respond in the way Ronald expected. Instead of sending in the big dollars he requested, they sent a delegation of special forces who took to the woods pursuing the robber band. Using their contact man very cautiously, they found out where the robber band was hiding, holed up on the top of a mountain south of Waslala toward a place called Yaró. As they kept up contact, supposedly preparing the money, the special forces located the mountain hideout and circled it, slowly but surely closing in.

Paco had plenty of time to do some deep thinking as he spent eleven days in the woods guarding Armando. Ronald came and went, but Paco and Ezequiel stayed put and watched the man they held hostage. Armando cooperated well, so they didn't even tie him up. The little bit of food that was brought in—often just tortillas—was shared by them all. Many times during those eleven days, Paco remembered his experience with the *gringos* in Kusulí. Many times, he found himself hating the job that he had on his hands. And, many times, he wondered if he would become a Christian again one day.

Paco knew God was trying to get a hold on his heart, but he wasn't quite ready to hear His voice. He pushed it off, saying, "Someday, I will get my heart right with the Lord again."

The morning was quiet, and not even the jungle birds were singing. Ronald had just arrived at the kidnapping scene with the other robber. "Boys, I have good news," Ronald bragged. "They are on their way. Today at noon, our contact man should come with the money. Dollars! Real dollars! And lots of them! Then we will turn you loose." He nodded to Armando. "And we will run."

Then it happened. The special forces attacked without warning. They rushed in through the brush, yelling and shooting high. Armando flopped down flat on the ground, his face tight against the soggy jungle leaves. The robbers ran, totally confused. Paco and Ronald both ran toward a gully on the Yaró side of the mountaintop. Just before they jumped over the edge of the vine-choked gully, a man jumped out in front of them shouting, "Stop!"

But the two robbers charged right on. Ronald flew down over the edge of the gully, unscathed. Paco also went down over the edge, but he carried something down with him, a bullet in his heart. He was dead before he stopped rolling through the jungle underbrush.

We can imagine Paco standing before the judgment seat of Christ. He hung his head before the King.

"Paco Artola, you are condemned to hell."

"But, God . . ."

"No. There are no buts. I gave you a wonderful opportunity to be saved just two weeks ago. I asked those poor missionaries in Waslala to shower my love on you through their lives. Do you even realize how costly that love is? Can you imagine how hard it was for them to do that? Pablo's wife was over at the house without her husband, weeping and praying. She suffered for a whole hour, surrounded by her children. She didn't know where you had taken her husband.

"Rosa gave her Bible away. I touched you through the brothers' words. You felt my Holy Spirit's conviction clearly. My angels put the thought in your mind that you could run up to them, throw your gun down, and repent, just like the Philippian jailor did when he heard songs in the night. You could have done it.

"I touched you with my costly love two weeks ago. And though I made you cry, you rejected it. The missionaries loved you and have been praying for you every day since, but you rejected that wonderful opportunity. Now you will have to pay the price of rejection. You must pay the price in full for rejecting such costly love. The price is hell for all eternity."

Rumble, rumble, rumble.

A truck made the bridge rumble as it roared overhead. Three young men sat on their haunches, under the bridge, smoking pot and talking. The Waslala night sky was totally clouded over. Three little red spots from their homemade cigars burned brightly in the dark, damp night. People, jeeps, and trucks crossed the bridge, and no one could see what was going on underneath it. Nor could anybody hear the words spoken.

The date was June 5,[12] The time, 7 p.m. It was five weeks since Ronald's robber band had hit the *gringos* in Kusulí and twenty-five days since they had kidnapped Armando.

"Paco died a horrible death," Fausto said in hushed tones.

Ezequiel nodded. "Of course, I didn't see it. I ran the opposite direction and didn't stay for the viewing," the young man chuckled. "But they say they got him right in his heart."

"And like always, Ronald got off scot-free, eh?"

"Yep. I'm sure he's somewhere in Costa Rica by now. That was his alternative plan. Slip over into Costa Rica to work and make money to go back to the U.S. I wonder if he made it."

---

12 *Read the missionaries' side of the story in Angels in the Night, chapter six.*

"What happened to the other robbers?" Fausto asked.

"I'm not sure. They say they have the contact man in jail, and I think the other fellow escaped too. He's probably off with Ronald. I'm sure glad they didn't get me. I could hear the bullets zipping above my head as I ran. They shot high at first because they didn't want to hit Armando. That's the only reason we escaped. After they saw Armando flatten down, they shot to kill. But, by then, I was hightailing it off that mountain like a scared cougar."

"How did they get Paco?"

"He ran head-on into one of the Special Forces coming up out of the gorge. It was peanuts to pick him off. He died right away."

"Man, I'm glad I wasn't along," Fausto sighed. His eyes were almost as bloodshot-red as the tip of his cigar. "I guess it's good that I had that fight with Ronald down by the *gringos*. That way he didn't invite me to go along. And it's good that this little squirt wasn't along either," Fausto threw in, turning toward the dark form of the teen-aged boy who smoked pot with them. It was too dark to see Ronald's youngest brother's expression. Even though his brother Paco had been killed and his oldest brother was a fugitive, Daniel hadn't changed his wicked ways. Though he was still a teenager, he was already as bold as some of the more seasoned robbers. He was clearly following in Ronald's footsteps.

"Hey, let's go down to the *gringos'* place tonight to get us some quick money," Ezequiel drawled. "I'm sick and tired of always being broke. How are we going to buy more weed?"

"Are you crazy?" Fausto answered, his mind foggy with the drug. "First of all, they won't have any money. Second, though I don't have much of a conscience left, the little I have really kicked up during that last robbery."

"Aw, come on!" Ezequiel insisted. "You said it is the easiest place in the world to steal, and they have lots of things we could sell for some quick money. You said that yourself."

"I'm not scared of those Yankees," Daniel threw in.

Fausto shook his head and took another draw on his cigar. "We do need money, but you'll have to come up with a better plan than that."

"Hey, what did you do with that Bible they were talking about?"

"I have it at Mama's place. I'm sure she reads it."

"Does she know where it came from?"

"Nope. I told her a lady gave it to me, and for once I told the truth, didn't I? I know I should be reading it. But I don't know. I don't think I could ever be a good Christian. It's just so hard to be good, isn't it?"

"We'll always be robber bums," Ezequiel agreed. "That's why I want to go to the *gringos* again. I will help you this time. They won't recognize you, and I'll take the blame. Come on. It will give us some quick, easy cash!"

"They don't have cash!"

"But I know where we can sell a radio or a stereo set in no time. . . ."

The debate lasted a full half hour. Slowly, Fausto yielded. His mind was numbed by the marijuana, and his desire for quick cash overpowered his better knowledge. The other two robbers won, and the *gringos'* sixteenth robbery was underway.

At 10 p.m. three bandits hid behind the same old banana patch. Though Fausto didn't really want to hit the *gringos* again, he was automatically the leader. He didn't cover his face; he didn't really care if they recognized him. Ezequiel had an old white hanky tied over the lower part of his face and a cap pulled down over his eyes. Daniel didn't wear a mask.

"Okay," Fausto schemed, "you, Daniel, will be the guard out by the guacamaya tree beside the house. If you see any light coming or hear any strange noises, you give us the owl call immediately. If we have to run, we run down behind the barn." Fausto pointed toward one of the dark buildings looming on the hilltop.

The two comrades nodded in the dark.

"Daniel, you will carry the machine gun. Don't be afraid to use it. We must be ready for anything."

"Hey, I want the pistol," Ezequiel demanded. "You know these people and aren't afraid of them."

"No," Fausto contradicted. "You take the knife. I will be the spokesman. And remember, just like Ronald told us the last time, no one is to hurt these people. We could get in deep trouble if we do."

"Don't be so superstitious," Ezequiel mocked. "You will be too sweet to them, and we won't get anything from them. I know what happened the last time!"

The boys were ready to head up to the house when Fausto called them back. "Hey, I forgot. Let's use nicknames tonight. We can't call each other by our real names. I am Culebra (snake) tonight. Only that, okay?"

"I will be Cara de Malo (bad face)." Ezequiel said.

"I won't need a nickname," Daniel reminded them. "I am staying outside anyway."

Minutes later, they were all gathered behind the *rancho* again. Fausto pointed out Daniel's tree, which had been cut down to a stump. "That's your position," Fausto whispered. Then, looking at Ezequiel, he clucked, "Ready? Let's go."

Fausto's drugged mind didn't feel the same fear it had five weeks before. Though in his heart he knew he was doing a very stupid thing, his fear was gone. He stepped out into the open, saying to himself, *I will be nice to them tonight. Very nice!*

The dog saw him as soon as he stepped out and ran toward him, barking ferociously.

"Don Pablo," Fausto hollered.

The window opened just like it had before. Fausto yelled, "Don Pablo, we want some food."

"Who is it?" a voice answered, muffled in sleep and surprise.

"Come on down, Don Pablo. We want to talk to you."

"Are you the same fellow who came last Friday?" Pablo asked apprehensively.

"No, but come on down. We need to talk to you."

"Okay. I'll be right down."

Fausto led the way as he and Ezequiel crossed the porch and stationed themselves by the door. Fausto decided not to pull out his pistol if it wasn't necessary. But Ezequiel, who stood in the background, drew his knife just in case.

Pablo opened the door and walked right over to Fausto. When Pablo stuck out his hand, Fausto wasn't surprised. He took it, and they shook hands warmly.

"Did you have robbers last Friday?" Fausto asked.

"Yes," Pablo answered. "It wasn't you?"

"No. We are the ones who came two months ago," Fausto answered honestly. "How much money do you have tonight?"

"Not much," Pablo said. "Maybe a hundred córdobas ($12)."

"Go get it." Fausto commanded.

When Pablo appeared again, Fausto took the money and stuck it in his pocket. Ezequiel wondered how much it was. He wanted to make sure he would get his share.

Then Fausto asked, "Where is that BB gun you showed me the last time? Go bring it."

Obediently, Pablo led the way into the office. Then, getting down on all fours, Pablo reached under the desk and pulled out the gun. *Wow, they know how to hide their things,* Fausto took note. "How does it work?"

Pablo pumped it several times and aimed at a sack of flour under the steps. *Ping!* The BB buried itself in the flour. "Lay the gun there," Fausto demanded, and Pablo laid it on the flour sack under the steps.

Then Fausto told Pablo to go outside on the porch to wait, and he obeyed. Ezequiel saw a little black howler monkey run over the porch floor. Pablo hunched down and caressed him and talked to him quietly.

"Base one. Base one." Daniel pretended to talk into a make-believe radio out on the stump.

Ezequiel was getting nervous, so he called out as quietly as he could, "Oye Culebra (hey, Snake)."

"Cara de Malo," Fausto answered, "come on in here."

The two robbers met in the living room, and Fausto led the way into the office. Knowing that Ezequiel was interested in the BB gun, he pointed to it in passing. Ezequiel grabbed it, feeling tougher with the familiar shape of a gun in his hands. Then they decided to take the radios. "That's where the easy cash is," Ezequiel reminded his buddy.

Fausto called Pablo in and insisted that he explain about the two radios that were in plain sight. Pablo admitted that they used the smaller one for calls within a close range, and the other was an expensive one they used to call to Costa Rica. Telling Pablo to go outside again, Fausto decided, *I'll take the small one.*

As Pablo slipped out of the office, Fausto stayed behind, disconnecting the radio. Ezequiel met Pablo in the living room on his way out. Hiding the BB gun behind his leg, Ezequiel motioned for him to stop, and then he whispered, "How much money did you give that guy?"

Pablo whispered back, "Just a hundred cords."

"Do you have a typewriter?" Ezequiel asked.

"Yes, I do," Pablo admitted. "It's not working right now. It needs a part. It's pretty big and clumsy."

"I want to see it," Ezequiel said.

Reluctantly, Pablo led the way upstairs and knocked softly on one of the doors, announcing himself to those within. As soon as someone opened the door, Pablo talked quietly to the people in the room in their language, clearly trying to put them at ease.

Ezequiel saw it all with one glance. The room was dark. Ezequiel shone his flashlight into the room, avoiding people's faces. A group of people sat around the edges of a bed. Ezequiel allowed the barrel of the BB gun to stick out. *So they think I am armed,* he thought nervously.

The woman of the house held a small girl on her lap. Her head was bowed, and he could tell she was afraid. But no one said a word. The atmosphere was tense, but Ezequiel didn't feel any panic. He noticed an electric iron perched on an ironing board in the corner.

Pablo pulled the big, heavy typewriter from a high shelf. He clunked it down on the floor. Ezequiel shone on the machine with his light. "Doesn't work at all?"

"Nope. It can be fixed, but it needs a part. But if you want it, you can have it."

"Let it go," Ezequiel decided. Then, pitying the woman and the children, he said, "Let's go."

When they got back down to the living room, Ezequiel met Fausto and whispered, "Hey, let's be careful. The lady of the house is pretty frightened." Then he turned to Pablo and commanded, "Go up and get me that iron."

Pablo went and brought it. Then Fausto told him to step outside again.

Daniel was wondering what all was happening in the large, dark house. He saw Pablo go in and come back out. He heard when Culebra and Cara de Malo called back and forth to each other. He saw the monkey run around nervously. But he had no idea what was going on. Now, seeing Pablo coming out on the porch again, he nervously cocked the machine gun he cradled in his hands. That caught Pablo's attention, and he walked toward him. Daniel was surprised, but not afraid.

"Good evening," Pablo said, hunching down beside him.

"Good evening," Daniel answered.

"What happened to the short, stocky fellow who came the last time? The one who wore the beret?"

My brother, Daniel thought. Though he hadn't been along on the kidnapping, he knew the details. He decided to be honest. "He got killed in a shootout."

"That's too bad," Pablo answered. Then the little black monkey showed up and rolled over onto his back in front of its owner. Pablo scratched its belly and the monkey shivered in delight.

"We love you guys," Pablo added. "We always hope that somehow through these robberies you will change your ways and find the Lord."

Daniel could hardly believe his ears. *I may be new to the stealing business, but this is unheard of. These people sure are strange,* he concluded. Changing the subject, he croaked, "Get me a glass of water."

Pablo went to the door and asked for permission to go in for the water. Fausto was going through the kitchen cabinets, so Pablo poured him a glass of water, too. Then Daniel saw him coming back, carrying a pitcher of cold water. As he received the glass of water, Daniel muttered, *"Gracias."*

Meanwhile, Fausto decided he wanted to see the typewriter. He went upstairs and shone the flashlight at the people huddled on the bed. The beam of light moved from one face to the next, but when it fell upon the face of the lady of the house, it stopped. Fausto's brain was clearing from the marijuana he had smoked hours earlier. The scene of the woman sitting there with her child on her lap and her head bowed low pierced his heart like a sword. *What am I doing?* He wondered. *I should not have come back to scare these poor people. God will punish me for this! I'm getting out of here!*

Taking a quick look at the typewriter, Fausto barked, "Let's go!" The typewriter stayed and the robber fled.

The robbery had lasted one hour. Now downstairs, the robbers quickly decided what they wanted to take. They wanted the large stereo set badly. "That is a family favorite," Pablo begged. "We got it cheap at a garage sale and we use it to listen to tapes."

But the robbers were in a hurry and turned deaf ears to his pleas. They packed the stuff into backpacks Pablo provided for them. Then Ezequiel asked, "Do you have some food for us?"

Pablo quickly gathered some food and handed it over. Ezequiel packed it into his bag, thanking Pablo profusely. Then Ezequiel almost cringed when Pablo put his hand on his shoulder. Fausto watched with a grin on his face. He knew what was coming. Hadn't he gotten the same treatment five weeks earlier? Pablo started slowly. *"Amigo,* I want to tell you about Jesus. He is my Saviour, and I love Him so much for what He did for me. I know He can do the same for you."

Ezequiel held perfectly still. Fausto was all ears, too. "We always hope that every time the robbers come they will somehow get a touch of God's love." Then, turning to Fausto, he continued, "And you, my friend, what have you done with Rosa's Bible?"

"I have it at my mother's place," Fausto responded.

"Have you been reading it?" Pablo asked in a tone a father might use with his son.

Fausto hung his head and answered, "Not much."

They all walked out onto the porch. Pablo shook hands with the two robbers and, again, gave them a blessing to take along home. At the stump, Daniel joined them. They walked down the lane together, their flashlights bobbing among the flitting fireflies.

The three robbers stopped on the road shortly after they left the *gringos'* house. "Let's grab a bite to eat," Ezequiel said. "Man, am I hungry!"

As Ezequiel unpacked the food, he quizzed Fausto. "Why are you so quiet? Is your conscience working on you again?"

"We're stupid to steal from these people. God is going to punish us."

"Look at this!" Ezequiel squealed. "Good food. Good cheese and some real *gringo* bread. And some cookies!"

Daniel was into feasting, too. Breaking off chunks of cheese and big pieces of bread, the men fell to eating. It wasn't long until Fausto was overcome by his hunger and took his share. "I am going to take some of this leftover cheese home to my mother," Daniel grinned, choking on his sandwich.

"Where will you tell her you got it?" Ezequiel asked.

"Oh, I don't know. I'll make up some kind of story. Look, these cookies sure are funny," Daniel chuckled. "Two chocolate cookies pasted together with white glue." Taking a bite, he smacked his lips and said, "These are the best cookies I have ever eaten, boys!"

Fausto ate, but his heart was not into the fun. After their starlit meal, he sighed. "I need a puff, boys."

His buddies saw that Fausto was not himself. They respected him for once and let him be. As they walked home, each was buried in his own thoughts—thoughts which seldom ran through robbers' minds. Thoughts about God. And thoughts and memories that would stay with them for many years.

When they got to Fausto's house, they decided to leave the radios and stereo set there until they were able to sell them. Ezequiel and Daniel took some of the other loot. Ezequiel, who didn't own a gun, took the BB gun. Fausto would return the borrowed machine gun to his brother, Jorge, sooner or later.

Fausto crept into his house like a mouse. Everyone was asleep. It was close to 1:30 a.m. when he hid the radios and the stereo set under his bed. Then he crawled under the covers and tried to sleep. But sleep wouldn't come. Every time he closed his eyes, he saw that gentle woman, her head bowed, fighting fear. He saw all the frightened children. Fear grew in his own heart. He knew God was angry with him. Finally, he crawled out of bed. Remembering how he'd prayed when he was converted years ago, he knelt by his bed and begged God for forgiveness for stealing from the *gringos*.

Old Wilfredo Sánchez stood in the middle of the living room with his hands on his hips. His wife and daughters cowered in different parts of the house. "What's going on?" Wilfredo bellowed, clearly angry. "I found a bunch of stuff under Fausto's bed. I was always afraid my boys were stealing, but now I'm sure. Not only that, they stole it from the *gringos*."

"How do you know it was from the *gringos?*" Wilfredo's daughter Carmen prodded.

"Come, look at this stereo set. No one in Waslala would have something like this. It is an American brand," Wilfredo barked, leading the way into his shop.

Wilfredo had a little shop to fix radios and stereo sets. A window opened right out to Waslala's main street. There on his work table, he had all the tools of his trade, and right in the middle of the table sat several radios and a big stereo set. "Look," Wilfredo growled. "That was stolen from the *gringos*, and that makes me ashamed. We hear all the time how those *gringos* get robbed and how they don't retaliate but leave everything in God's hands. That's why I know they are God's people. Now to think that my boys are doing this makes me angry. Very angry!"

Old Wilfredo boasted of having served the Lord for almost forty years. Being an honest working man, it was awfully hard for him to accept the fact that his boys were turning out to be robbers. Shaking his head, he commanded, "Carmen, I want you to go to the *gringos'* house tomorrow and tell them the stuff is here at our place and that they should come get it."

"But we could get in trouble with the police!" Carmen said anxiously. "We can't afford to do that."

Wilfredo thought for a bit. "Well, Carmen, make up some story about how you found the stuff. You don't have to say your brothers stole it. Just make sure they come and get their stuff back. I'll talk to Fausto myself as soon as he comes home."

Wilfredo put the stolen things away and sat down again at his work table. As he fixed an old radio for a friend, his mind wandered far from his job. *Why have my boys turned out this way? What went wrong? I taught them about the Lord. I taught them to fear God. I did not teach them to steal.* Old Wilfredo's heart burned as his mind recalled the scenes of his past.

Jorge, my oldest son, was always a rebel. No, he wasn't a robber back in those days. But he always had a hard time submitting to me. And I had an anger problem that didn't help the situation. Thank the Lord that He has been changing me. But it is too late to salvage my boys. They lost respect for me because I got so angry and beat them for their disobedience.

Then the war started. That's what changed it all. Jorge joined the counter-revolution. Vicente and Fausto were too young to join, and because of the rough times we were facing, they turned to the Lord. Oh, those were the good days! Wilfredo felt tears push their way up under his eyelids. *Vicente and Fausto both were so on fire for the Lord. Oh, how they prayed! They witnessed, and Vicente especially wanted to be a minister someday.*

But then the war ended and Jorge came home. The boys were fascinated with his gory stories. I tried to warn them. They discovered that Jorge and his cronies had caches of arms hidden away. Their cousin, Ronald, sure didn't help the situation. He and Jorge were so bold. Slowly, but surely, Vicente and Fausto lost their faith and followed these men's ways.

Jorge and Ronald had learned that if they approached a house with machine guns, everybody melted and gave them what they wanted. Who would stand up to the feared AK 47 machine guns? That's the way my boys learned to steal. Now I can't get them to work at all. They spend their days sleeping and their nights running around. Wilfredo shook his head sadly and prayed to God.

That night when Fausto came home after 10 p.m. his dad was already asleep. But Carmen met him at the back door. "Fausto," she whispered, "be careful. Father is very angry. He found some things under your bed."

"Oh," Fausto grunted. "So I'm in trouble?"

"Kinda," Carmen answered. "Not only does he suspect that they are stolen, but he thinks you got the stuff at the *gringos*. Did you?"

Fausto nodded. "We've gone there twice. But I will never do it again. They are godly people, and I am afraid."

"That's what Father says. He is ashamed that you would steal from those poor people. He says they have probably been robbed ten times already," Carmen added, her eyes big in the dark.

"Sixteen times, to be exact!" Fausto nodded seriously. "And two of those times it was me. But I asked God to forgive me. I haven't even felt like selling the stuff. What is Father going to do about it?"

Carmen looked at her brother closely. *Should I tell him?* She decided to give it a try. "I am supposed to go tell the *gringos* tomorrow to come and get their stuff."

To Carmen's surprise, Fausto hung his head and said, "That's fine. Go do it. But don't tell them who did it. You will have to come up with some story so they don't think it was us. Tell them you found it in the weeds somewhere."

"Right," Carmen agreed. "I will make the things soaking wet so they will believe my story. I will be ready for tomorrow."

"I'm getting out of here. Thanks for warning me. I'll be gone before Father wakes up in the morning."

The next day, a bus stopped in front of the *gringo's* farm, and a short, chunky girl with wavy hair crawled off the bus. The bus roared away, and she walked in the long lane slowly. As she walked, she polished her story more and more. Hesitantly, she approached the *gringo's* house.

"*Buenas.*"

Carmen had often seen the *gringos* go past their house on the street, but she had never talked to them personally. Now, with a friendly "*Buenas,*" Pablo walked across the porch to meet her. After shaking her hand, he asked, "And what can I do for you?"

"I need to talk to you in private," she whispered nervously. "Could we talk?"

"Sure," Pablo answered wonderingly. "Let's step over here to the back of the house."

When they had rounded the corner, Pablo turned to give Carmen his full attention. She started to unwind her tale. "The other day, as my sister and I were washing in the creek," she said, "we looked up and saw two strange men sneaking down over the hill, carrying a sack of stuff. They were acting suspicious, so we ducked down behind the bank before they could see us. We watched them disappear into the brush close to where we were. Soon they came out, looking around warily. They didn't see us, so they left. We noticed that they didn't have their sack anymore. So we suspected they were robbers hiding their loot."

Pablo watched Carmen's face as she talked. "Did you recognize the guys?" Pablo asked.

"No," Carmen lied again. "They were total strangers. We washed for hours, and they didn't return. So we sneaked into the brush and found the sack. It had a radio and a stereo set in it. But we didn't take it. We were too afraid. We ran home and told our father. The next day he told us to check to see if it was still there. If it was, he asked us to bring it home. So we did."

Pablo looked at the girl incredulously. "Wow!"

Carmen continued with her yarn. "It rained hard that night. The stuff got soaked. My father saw right away that the stereo set was American. He said, 'The only people who would have a nice set like this are the *gringos*.' Was he right?"

"Yes," Pablo answered slowly. "The robbers took a radio and a stereo set several weeks ago."

"That's what we thought. You can come pick up the stuff anytime."

"Well, thanks so much! What do I owe you?"

"No, nothing. I am not trying to make money off you. I just want to make sure the stuff gets back to its rightful owner, that's all."

"Thank you very much! Let me talk to my wife. Maybe I will just go to Waslala right away. How did you come?"

"I came on the bus."

Pablo disappeared into the house. Carmen waited. Soon he was back. "I'll just go to Waslala right away to pick up the stuff. You can ride along with me."

As the two bounced their way toward Waslala in the white jeep, Carmen and Pablo visited. She was so glad that Pablo didn't probe more into what had happened. Now she could understand what her father meant when he said the *gringos* were nice people.

When they got to Don Wilfredo Sánchez's place, Wilfredo disappeared into the kitchen. He did not want to be interrogated about how the things got to his house, and he knew Carmen could handle the situation by herself. Carmen showed Pablo the stash in her father's shop. "Sure enough," Pablo grinned. "The stuff is ours. And I can see it was soaked in the rain. Well, I am glad God willed that we got it back. That's all I can say."

Carmen nodded. Then Pablo reached into his pocket and pulled out a hundred córdoba bill. "I know you aren't charging me for getting these things back, but I want to give you a little gift expressing my gratitude. My children will be so happy to have their tape player back. My wife often listens to songs when she is sad or afraid because of the robbers. It helps encourage her."

"Thanks," Carmen said, accepting the gift.

"May God bless you!" Pablo responded. Then he picked up his things and left.

After he drove away, Don Wilfredo, his wife, and Carmen met at the office. They discussed the situation for a long time. Carmen told her father how Fausto admitted he had made a bad mistake and that he had promised not to bother the *gringos* again.

"Pablo told me that his wife listens to hymns on the stereo set when she is sad or afraid of the robbers," Carmen told them.

"To think that our son is partly the reason she is so afraid," Wilfredo interjected.

"I sure pity that lady, especially when I hear that they have been robbed sixteen times," Wilfredo's wife sighed.

Wilfredo closed the conversation by saying, "I'm glad they at least got some of their things back. May God bless them."

Two months later, Jorge and Vicente showed up in Waslala again. Soon after they were back, Jorge heard about a rich farmer who had sold a batch of cattle up on Papayo Hill. He called

Fausto and Vicente together for a pow-wow. "Let's hit the guy tonight before he reinvests his money," Jorge suggested.

"I'd rather not," Fausto retorted. "It's too close. Those guys might recognize us, and *wham-o,* we'd be in jail."

"Naw," Jorge drawled. "We'll be careful. I'll be the leader. You guys just go along to help. It's good money and fairly easy, too."

"I don't agree," Fausto argued. "It's too dangerous. It's easy for you because you are leaving the area again. But I live here. I'm not going this time unless you plan a robbery farther away."

The three argued for a while, Vicente siding with Fausto. So Jorge gave up and did the robbery with two other Waslala bums. Jorge masked himself well, but the young hoodlums didn't. They pulled off the robbery and ran with the money. Jorge skipped the country like usual, but the farmer recognized one of the other boys. The police caught the young fellow, and it didn't take much pressure to make him confess. "It was the Sánchez boys," was all he would say.

The police hit at five in the morning. Fausto and Vicente were still in bed when the police pounded on their door. Don Wilfredo opened willingly and sadly watched as they handcuffed his two sons and hauled them off at gun point. At the police station the two boys declared their innocence, but to no avail. "The judge will decide if you participated in that robbery or not," the head policeman barked. "We are sending you to La Perrera (Dog Pen—a prison in Matagalpa). If you are innocent, you will soon be free."

Fausto and Vicente were in the Waslala jail for three days while the officials prepared the case to send to Matagalpa. During that time Fausto had time to think. He appreciated his parents. Though they were upset at his doings, they still loved him and brought him food twice a day.

On the second day, Fausto started to think about God. He considered praying, but wasn't sure if he was worthy to cry out to a holy God. Then he remembered Rosa's Bible. He sent his mother a note, and that evening the Bible came to him along with his food.

When Fausto saw the Bible, he took it into his hands tenderly. He opened the zipper and admired the nice, clean pages. Then he closed it respectfully and put it with his things. His heart wasn't ready yet to absorb its message. Although he didn't know it then, he would have plenty of time to do that later.

The third day, the police sent the two boys to Matagalpa and straight to La Perrera.

———

The sky was still inky black, with only a hint of pink on the horizon, due east. The gnarled old eucalyptus tree's leaves hung perfectly still, like strands of hair hanging from a moppy head. A rufous-naped wren stuck its head out from under a cluster of the eucalyptus leaves, peeping to see if it was time to begin a delightful song to the dawn. Seeing that it was still a bit too early, it pulled its head back in and tucked it under its wing again. It would be a shame to disturb the hush on the hill yet.

The cold cement jail called La Perrera waited in silence. Within minutes, the cooks would be up, stoking the fires and making the first batch of coffee for the day. But not yet. A hundred and twenty prisoners were still curled up in their thin blankets on their cement beds; sleeping as well as they could in the predawn cold.

The hush was more than a natural hush; it was the hush of God. No one knew what the Holy Spirit was planning that morning; even the prisoners didn't realize what they were waiting on or what their hearts yearned for. In His love and mercy, God looked down upon them and whispered, "Your day has come."

God had heard the prayers of His precious daughter named Rosa. Every day she had been praying, "God, please use my Bible to save some souls."

That eventful morning, as the whole hill lay in silence, God saw the Bible tucked away in Fausto's battered knapsack. The Holy Spirit knew that this day the Bible would be brought out. That anointed Book, empowered by many prayers from a distant place called Kusulí, would change the lives of many prisoners who lay curled up in their misery. Indeed, their day of deliverance had come.

Fausto awoke slowly. He realized anew where he was, and his heart fell. In jail. Who knew for how long? Vicente had been released the second day after they were brought to this horrible place. But here he was in cell number eight with forty other prisoners.

Later, after a meager breakfast of a little rice and one tortilla, Fausto had nothing to do. The sun was up now, baking the tin roof and whatever was beneath it. Fausto sat cross-legged on his cement bed, his head hanging low. His case was proceeding very slowly; he felt doomed. *I know I deserve to be in jail,* Fausto mused. *If only it weren't for this stupid robbery, which I didn't even help with! Now Jorge is scot-free, and I have to sit here and rot. Who knows when I will get out?*

Then he remembered the Bible. Reaching behind him, he pulled his satchel forward and opened the zipper. He pulled out the Bible and held it in his hands reverently. Slowly, he opened the zipper and stared at the page. He didn't read—just sat there on the edge of his bed and thought. He remembered that strange night when he had acquired the book.

Memories raced through his brain, and he again felt shame for what he had done. He remembered the woman who had given him the book. As he had ripped her house apart, she had sat out on the porch, singing. In his mind he could still see her, wearing that long dress and that white cloth on her head. He remembered her smile when she handed him the Bible and said, "Yes, you can have the Bible gladly."

Suddenly Fausto heard a quiet voice above him. Looking up, he saw a dark-skinned man leaning over the edge of the top bunk, staring at the Bible.

"Is that your Bible?" he asked.

"Yes," Fausto answered. "Do you like it?"

"Yes, I do," he whispered. "See, I am a Christian."

"Why are you here then?" Fausto asked, eyeing the man hunched up on his bunk.

"I—I have a stepson," he sighed. "We don't get along. One day I lashed him. The neighbors saw it and turned me in. He had marks on his body, and they stuck me in here."

"Where are you from?" Fausto asked the middle-aged man.

"I'm from Dario. I am a deacon in our church. I don't know how long they will keep me in here. Will you let me read the book?"

"Sure," Fausto answered, handing the Bible up to him.

Fausto lay back on his cot and his mind continued its musings. To his surprise, the man started reading out loud. He started reading from the book of Revelation. "The Revelation of Jesus Christ, which God gave unto him, to shew unto his servants things which must shortly come to pass" (Revelation 1:1).

A hush fell over the forty prisoners as the deacon read the Bible. The man found courage from deep within his heart and read louder. Soon the Bible reading had caught the attention of the whole cell. This was the Word of God.

Fausto shared his Bible with the deacon that day and the next. The third day was a Sunday. To the surprise of everyone in the cell, the deacon got up and stood in the center of the room and started to read from Revelation loudly and clearly. Then, surprising even himself, he started preaching salvation through Jesus Christ.

As he preached, the prisoners found their shirts and put them on. Some who'd been lounging around in their shorts found their pants. For some reason it seemed proper to be dressed while this man preached.

One of the first things the deacon did was explain why he was in jail. "I know I should have been gentler with the boy, but it still wasn't near bad enough to pen me up. I am an active deacon in my home church, and I am ashamed that I have had to come to this awful place. But God has a purpose in having me here, and I have just discovered what it is. I feel God calling me to preach in this cell. I want to thank Fausto Sánchez for letting me use his Bible." Then, raising the book high, he exclaimed, "This book contains the Way of Life, and I am going to preach it until the day God takes me home."

That first sermon was preached in power, and the Holy Spirit used the power of the Word to touch lives. Fausto listened well. His desire for God grew. The hearts in cell number eight were ready for the Word. By the time the deacon was done preaching, a lot of his cellmates were thinking, and some were even praying. That first message set the stage for the unique revival God was bringing into La Perrera.

During that first message, one of the guards tried to quiet the deacon down. "Shut up, you preacher!" he barked. "It's illegal to preach in the cells." But the other prisoners hooted at the guard until he left them alone. The deacon preached on.

The Bible had been brought in by a criminal and had landed in the hands of a repentant deacon. As the Word was proclaimed, others started reading and preaching, and revival was well on the way.

While Fausto was in cell eight, a wicked criminal landed in
La Perrera because of kidnapping and big-time robbery. He
was white-skinned, tall, and strongly built. Not only was he
a criminal, he was a sexual pervert. As soon as he entered the
cell, he let people know who he was. Even Fausto blushed because he was so ashamed. But after several days, the prisoners in cell eight decided they simply had to accept the wicked
young man as he was. The first time the deacon preached, the
man sat in the corner with a mocking grin on his face. But he
was a prisoner—he had no option but to listen.

One night after hearing a message on the love of God, Fausto
couldn't sleep. His heart ached from his horrible sins, and the
love of God moved him. But a serious problem held him back.
The battle raged in his heart for hours as he tossed on his cold
cement bed. *I do not want to become a Christian just because I am
trapped in this dungeon. I have to be real. If I do it now and then get
out soon, I will go right back to the life I led before. If I do it now, it
will just be so that God gets me out of here. I will wait.*

The distraught man fought on. Finally, he found a measure
of peace when he made his vow. *Lord, if You get me out of here, I
will seek You and serve You faithfully until the end. I am not going
to do it now just because I am in this crisis. But I will do it later with
all my heart. Then I will prove that I will serve You even when I am
not behind these bars.*

Even the prisoners of the cells nearby took interest. One day,
a man from the cell across the aisle hollered, "Please let us use
the Bible, too. A brother here says he can preach if he has a
Bible."

Fortunately, a friendly guard who was sympathetic to the
revival was on duty that day. He passed the Bible over to the
next cell, and minutes later, a man in the next cell was preaching.

One evening the deacon was preaching again. A quiet man was sitting on his bunk, and Fausto could see that he was being touched. Before long, the man threw his blanket over his head to hide his face. Everybody could hear him sobbing under his blanket. When the deacon gave an invitation, the man stuck his hand out from under the blanket. The deacon invited him to come to the center of the cell and prayed for him.

After this quiet man was converted, he confessed that he used to be an evangelist of the Word but had fallen away. He had gotten involved in cattle business and had bought a bunch of stolen cattle. That was why he was in prison. Right there, he promised to serve the Lord until the day he died.

A few weeks after the deacon had started preaching, he received a summons. Soon they brought him back, rejoicing. As he came into the cell to get his things, he shouted, "Praise the Lord! I am free!"

His cellmates cheered for him as he left the cell, promising to pray for the prisoners. He tenderly gave the Bible back to Fausto and announced, "Someone needs to start preaching in my place. Keep the revival going!"

The quiet gentleman picked up the preaching naturally. In spite of harassing and mocking from the unfriendly guard and some hard-hearted inmates, the preaching continued, and more souls were saved. Fausto fought boredom and discouragement with his case, but he felt a certain joy in his heart that his Bible was being moved from cell to cell. Every day, he could hear some voice preaching from the book. He began keeping track of the number of souls saved in his cell.

Several weeks later, the quiet man was released too. Other converted men took the Bible and read it. A hush always fell upon the prisoners as the Word was read. Soon, the converted ones were holding full-fledged services every night. The men would sing and clap for a full half-hour before the preaching started.

During that time the perverted man seemed to calm down. One day he walked up to Fausto and asked. "May I read your Bible?"

Fausto let him read it. After reading for a time, he sat for a while as if stunned. Then a brother preached a message about God's love for sinners. The big man started to weep. No one in the cell knew what to do for this poor, crying child trapped in the body of a big, strong man. Fausto was moved, but felt helpless. He just looked on as others tried to help.

The man cried off and on for three whole days.

One Sunday afternoon the service started at 3 p.m. After preaching a powerful message, a convert opened the service for testimonies. Many of the converts testified to what Christ had done to them in the last several weeks on the hill of La Perrera. Suddenly the big sinner came forward and said, "I want to accept Christ as my Saviour."

The whole cell cheered and the brethren prayed with him. After he was converted, others came forward and asked to be saved. It seemed as if the whole cell was struck by God. Time went on, and man after man came forward, asking for prayer. At ten o'clock there were no more converts to pray for. Over half of the men in the cell were Christians now, so the inmate who was preaching led the men in a time of praise and worship. The singing and rejoicing went on until midnight.

After two months and twenty-three days, Fausto was finally called into court. During an hour-long ordeal, it was proven that he was not involved in the robbery. He went back to cell eight one more time to pick up his things. An inmate who was using the Bible to preach was reading the Bible when he stopped in.

"May I have my Bible?" Fausto asked.

"Please," the man begged earnestly. "You know this Bible has been such a blessing in this cell. I don't think you should take it. It's like it belongs here. So many men have been converted here in this cell."

"Forty-seven, to be exact," Fausto confirmed.

"You can always buy another Bible. This jail really needs this one," the inmates insisted.

It became clear to Fausto that he would have to leave without his Bible. He said goodbye to his friends with mixed feelings. Though he still hadn't given his heart to the Lord, the experiences in cell eight had a powerful effect on his life, and he would never be able to doubt the power of the Bible again.

Just one Bible, anointed with the power of the Holy Ghost! As Rosa had given her Bible to Fausto, now he passed it on, and it became cell eight's Bible. But all along, it was God's Bible, and it would surely serve His purpose.

————————

After the experiences in La Perrera, Fausto tried hard to reform. During the next year, true to his vow, he made a commitment to God and was baptized in an Evangelical church, where he became an active member. He lived at home with his parents.

Soon after that, Fausto married a girl from Casca, a remote village where his family had lived when he was born. Sandra was from a family they had known during his growing up years, but she did not know the life Fausto had lived later while living in Waslala.

Fausto brought his new wife to Waslala, and they lived with his parents. Soon they had a son whom they named Jeffrey. After several years passed, Fausto fell back into his life of sin and forgot his vows to the Lord. He started drinking and doing drugs. Then, always needing money, he started stealing again.

During the time he was converted, he had learned to play the trumpet and would play during the services whenever he had a chance. Just before he fell back into sin, a pastor gave him a used trumpet which was still in good shape. After that, Fausto started singing in a worldly mariachi band. This group of men not only sang together, but they also drank and partied together whenever they had an opportunity.

One morning the weather was cloudy. A big rain was creeping over Papayo Hill and sneaking in on Waslala. Fausto had gone to the market to get some vegetables for his mother. He walked down the street with the bag of vegetables in his hand at the same pace as the rest of people who swarmed the streets of Waslala on a Friday.

To his dismay, he noticed the *gringos'* white Land Cruiser jeep parked by the road up ahead. Pablo was walking away from the back of his jeep where he had just weighed a chunk of cheese to deliver to the store across the sidewalk. Fausto's heart froze when he saw their paths were going to meet. But instead of stopping or trying to hide, making it obvious, he decided to walk on with the rest of the crowd as if nothing were amiss. *Maybe he won't recognize me.*

Sure enough, just as Fausto walked past, Pablo stepped away from the jeep, the flapjack cheese balanced on his hand. Pablo paused to let Fausto pass on the sidewalk. As Fausto passed, he kept Pablo in his view out of the corner of his eye. Briefly, ever so briefly, their eyes met. Fausto saw not the smallest sign of recognition. After walking on by, Fausto looked back. Pablo was disappearing into the store, totally oblivious that he had just made eye contact with one of his robbers.

Fausto relaxed, chiding himself. *Why did I think he would recognize me? Today I am dressed neatly. That night I wore old, dark clothes and rubber boots. That night it was dark, and he probably never saw my face clearly. Today he sees my face in broad daylight and never dreams that I am the same man. Neat!* He grinned. *Now I don't have to worry about meeting them like I used to.*

Fausto was a little tipsy. He and his four cronies had just started what was going to be a wild Sunday night. They'd had their first drinks and were walking down one of Waslala's back streets on their way to Esquina Caliente (Hot Corner), where the booze ran freely and where the wild Waslala men usually ended up on a Sunday evening.

Suddenly Juanito, one of Fausto's buddies, stopped in his tracks, causing Fausto to walk smack into him. With an oath, Fausto grabbed him and yelled, "What's wrong, man?"

Juanito was pointing. Right beside the road was a church house. People were crowded up to the wide door, and some even stood at the windows. "Preaching," Juanito belched.

They could hear the preacher's voice blaring out of a loud-speaker. Fausto laughed. "Let's go in and hear what the preacher has to say."

Soon the five men were walking up the sidewalk toward the doorway packed with people. Two clean-cut young men immediately ushered them into the building. Fausto was not ready for that. He'd expected to hug the outskirts and peer through the windows like the street kids. But these young men had other plans. The next thing the five men knew, they were inside the building, toward the back, comfortably seated in a church pew.

What shocked Fausto most wasn't the fact that they were suddenly in the center of a worship service, when minutes before they had been carousing. What shocked him was the speaker. It was none other than Pablo, the *gringo! This must be their church building,* Fausto mused, looking around. He could see that it was a special service and that a lot of people had come out to listen. Pablo was preaching about an alternative for Nicaragua.

Fausto was tipsy, but far from drunk. He understood the message perfectly. "What Waslala needs is not more religion,"

Pablo announced with conviction. "What Waslala needs are men and women who will give their all for Jesus."

Remembering his own religious experience, Fausto knew that it was true. "So many of you are playing games with God; you say, 'Lord, Lord,' but your hearts are far from Him. You don't even want to obey Him anymore. God hates your mediocrity!" Fausto was seen nodding, totally engrossed.

As he listened, he remembered all the things he had done against the preacher and his family. He found himself blushing. *What if that man recognizes me? I know he speaks the words of God.*

After listening to the message for half an hour, Fausto got nervous. Juanito was whimpering. He leaned over to Fausto and whispered too loudly, "Let's go forward during the invitation."

Fausto knew Juanito was even tipsier than he was. It would do no good to go forward in the condition they were in. Moreover, Fausto was embarrassed at the way Juanito was crying.

"You can repent tonight. You can come to Jesus and give Him your all. He loves you so much. He gave His only begotten Son for you. What are you waiting for?" Pablo preached his heart out.

Fausto knew the invitation was coming soon. Juanito was crying harder and insisting, "Fausto, let's go forward. I want to be saved. I will, if you will."

Fausto had to make a decision soon. All of his buddies looked to him as their leader. It looked as if Juanito would go forward drunk, and that would be the unthinkable. Suddenly Fausto knew what he had to do. Get out of there. Fast. Winking at his buddies, he got to his feet. Juanito got up quickly, thinking they were going forward. Fausto whispered into his ear, "Let's go."

All five men filed out of the church house. The devil cheered. But God knew that the Holy Spirit would use Pablo's words to continue His work in their hearts. Especially in Fausto's.

———————

"Fausto," Sandra called out, "the lady we buy milk from didn't have any milk left by the time I got there this morning. What can we do? We have to have milk for Jeffrey's bottle."

Fausto was sharpening his machete behind the house and did not feel like going anywhere for milk. "What *can* we do? There is just no milk," he grumbled.

"They say the *gringos* sell milk," was Sandra's quick answer. "Please go buy at least a little to hold us over. If I go earlier, I know the lady will have milk for me tomorrow."

"I don't want to go to the *gringos'* place," Fausto growled.

"Why not? They're nice people."

"I just don't want to, that's all."

"Are you allergic to *gringos?*" Sandra insisted.

Half an hour later, Fausto was walking up the street toward the *gringos'* place carrying a plastic jug. As he walked, he wondered what would happen if he had to meet Pablo and talk to him. Would Pablo recognize him then?

As Fausto topped the hill, he saw a brightly-painted building on the right side of the street. Beside it was a wide entrance with the gate hanging open. Pablo had sold his place at Kusulí due to the robberies and had moved to this little piece of land. *Maybe it's partly my fault that they moved out here,* Fausto mused.

After walking up the gravel lane and making several zigzags, Fausto found himself approaching a house with a thick covering of ivy vines creeping up its cement walls. Beyond the house stood the barn, where Fausto could see several cows being milked. Several children loitered around the barn waiting for their milk. Speeding up his pace, he skirted the house and walked toward the barn. His heart was thumping a little harder than usual as he approached the barn and said, *"Buenas."*

To his surprise, Pablo himself walked out of the barn to meet him. "So you want some milk?" Pablo asked kindly.

"Yes," Fausto answered quickly. He could see that Pablo hadn't recognized him. Fausto relaxed as Pablo took his bottle and filled it with milk. He noticed several of Pablo's children helping with the milking. He recognized the oldest son as the one in the bedroom, whom they had frightened during the night of the robbery.

"Here's your milk," Pablo answered cheerfully, handing him the bottle. "That will be six córdobas."

As Fausto took the jug of milk, their eyes met briefly. The look meant nothing to the *gringo*, but it was like a shock to Fausto's heart. As he walked out the lane, memories of those two nights haunted him all the way home and visited his dreams that night.

During the year Fausto and Sandra lived in Waslala, Fausto went to buy milk at Pablo's farm three times. The other two times he met up with only Pablo's hired man and some of Pablo's children.

Every time Fausto saw any of the Yoder family, they vividly reminded him of his horrid past. And though he told no one, in his heart he longed to be like them.

Even as he longed for peace, Fausto still followed Satan and lived a life of sin. But during this whole time, he could never shake off what had happened in La Perrera and the vow he had made there. Would his dream to be a real Christian ever come true?

After living several more years in sin, Fausto again reconciled in an evangelical church. His wife was so happy, and even little Jeffrey could tell a difference in his daddy. Fausto's life changed, and his vices dropped like loosened shackles from his soul and mind. Finally Fausto was happy and on his way to real freedom. Then one night he had a dream.

Fausto was walking down a wide, spacious street in awe. On either side were beautiful, tall buildings. Some were at least a hundred stories high. Fausto had never been in a city like that before. He had never seen anything so glorious and awesome.

As Fausto walked down the street, he noticed that he was alone. *Where am I, and what is this beautiful place? Is it heaven? No, it can't be heaven. Heaven won't look like this.*

Suddenly he noticed a man walking down the street toward him. As he got closer to the man, he recognized him, and his heart lurched in his chest. It was the preacher, Pablo. Feeling guilty, he searched for a place to hide. But there was no place to hide. *I will just walk past nonchalantly like I used to in Waslala, and he won't recognize me at all.*

Fausto walked on, but things did not go as he expected. The man swerved to meet him and stopped, forcing Fausto to face him. Fausto's heart beat wildly in his chest. It was too late to run. But his heart slowed down when he saw that Pablo was smiling. Pablo slowly lifted his hand and pointed his finger right at Fausto's face. "I know who you are," he said simply.

Fausto was trembling all over now, expecting Pablo to get angry and start shouting at him for frightening his family and stealing his things. But Pablo just stood there and smiled at him. "How do you know who I am?" Fausto asked fearfully.

Pablo shook his finger at him again and answered kindly, "God gave me a gift. I can look at someone and know who he is. You are Fausto, and you visited our house twice way back in 1997."

Fausto hung his head in shame. He did not try to argue nor defend himself. He knew it was useless. So he changed the subject. "Pablo, where are we, and what is this city?"

Pablo swung his arm out over the vast city and said wistfully, "This is the kingdom of God, brother."

Then Fausto awoke from his dream, his heart thumping against his chest. A beautiful feeling washed over him. *Pablo has forgiven me. I don't have to be afraid of him anymore. Maybe I will meet him soon, and he will recognize who I am.*

Kneeling beside his bed, Fausto started to pray. In his prayer he mentioned Pablo's name. Then he got up and told his wife parts of the dream. But he was careful not to tell her that he had robbed the *gringos* years before.

Two weeks later Fausto saw his brother, Vicente, walking the path toward his house. Eagerly he jumped up to meet him. He knew that Vicente had become a Christian four years earlier. But why would Vicente come all the way back into Casca to see him? Since Vicente lived in Jinotega, a day's bus ride from Waslala, Fausto hardly ever saw him. The times they had met, Fausto had witnessed to him briefly and encouraged him to change his life by seeking Christ. Now, for the first time, he would meet his younger brother as a Christian.

After shaking hands and catching up on general family news, Fausto motioned to a chair and asked, "What brings you back here, my brother?"

"I am here on a special mission," Vicente smiled. "I wonder what you will think of it."

"What's up?" Fausto grinned.

"Are you serving the Lord?" Vicente asked.

"Absolutely! I have been faithful for a year now. It has not been easy for me, but I have finally gotten on my feet spiritually."

"Then you will like my mission," Vicente rejoiced. "Guess who sent me here."

"I can't. Just tell me."

"Pablo Yoder from Waslala."

Fausto eyes bulged, and he sat up straight. "What does he want? Does he know about me?"

"Yes, he does. Our cousin told him about us. But Pablo is not angry. Our cousin had told him that Jorge and I participated too, so Pablo went all the way to Jinotega and looked me up, and then we went together and found Jorge in San Rafael del Norte. We explained that, though we were also big-time robbers, we never visited them."

"What in the world does he want?"

"He is writing a book. He has written several books which tell the Yoders' testimony of how God protected them during the robber days in Kusulí. Now he says that God has been showing him who some of the robbers were who came to steal."

Fausto nodded knowingly. "It's a gift God gave him."

"He is writing their stories in a book. But he says he is sad because most of the ones they found out about are dead. Now he is excited to learn that maybe one of them is converted. Jorge and I both agreed to give our testimonies. We told him everything. I even told him how I shot that fellow who was trying to kill Jorge years ago. I told him I have one dead man on my back, you have two, and that Jorge can't even count how many men he killed. He was grateful for our willingness to share our testimonies, but he can't use them in the book because we never visited them. He is only taking testimonies of those who actually stole from them. That's why he wants your testimony badly. Will you give it?"

"Yes, I will," Fausto agreed immediately. "I had a dream, and now I see how it is coming true."

"He wants me to take you out to Waslala tomorrow. He will pay your bus fare. He wants to meet you."

"I will go to Waslala," Fausto said, with remorse in his tone. "I am ashamed of the deeds I did, but I am willing to let him use my testimony in his book. I will tell him the whole story. I will tell him the truth. Yes, tomorrow we will go to Waslala."

Fausto and Carmen walked the gravel lane slowly. She knew what was happening. All the family did, except for his wife, Sandra. Pablo had visited Old Wilfredo, and he had agreed to help set up this meeting. He had recommended that Vicente be the in-between man. Now Vicente was running an errand, and Carmen was taking Fausto to Pablo's place.

Fausto remembered walking in the same lane to buy milk. So, when they approached the immaculate lawn and well-kept grounds, he was not surprised. His sister called out, because she was afraid of Pablo's dogs. Then Pablo himself walked across the yard, wearing a big smile on his face. Pablo greeted Fausto's sister first and shook her hand, thanking her for bringing Fausto. Then he turned and met Fausto's eyes. As they shook hands, their eyes clung to each other. Fausto felt himself blushing. But even as his heart sped up and his arteries swelled, he knew he had nothing to be afraid of. Pablo eyes were just as kind as they had been thirteen years earlier when he had given them food and served them coffee in Kusulí. Fausto knew he was in good hands.

Pablo waved goodbye to Carmen and invited Fausto over to a *rancho* by a pond. He asked Fausto to sit at a table that was waiting in the center of the little building. Beside the *rancho* in the middle of the pond was Monkey Island where two monkeys swung around in their tree. It was a peaceful place, and Fausto relaxed.

Before long, Fausto found himself chatting with this friendly man as if they were old friends. At one point, he looked at Pablo and confessed sadly, "Yes, I did visit you when you lived in Kusulí. I am ashamed of what we did, but you know, that's the way it is when you serve Satan. I—"

"Just a minute," Pablo interrupted. "Would you mind if I recorded this session?"

"No; no problem," Fausto answered.

Pablo pulled out a tiny black box from his pocket, pushed some buttons, and laid it on the table. Then, also taking a seat, Pablo started. "Well, here we are. As you well know, we have to do this sharing session in total confidence. I have to trust you that you are sincere, because you could use this to get close to me to steal from me again. And you have to trust me that I won't use this information to stick you in jail. But that is not why we are here, right?"

Fausto nodded vigorously. "We trust each other."

"Fausto, I want to tell you that, though we suffered intensely in Kusulí, God blessed us much. He protected us during all those robberies. Now I feel a calling to write this book about what happened to our robbers."

Fausto nodded.

"Fausto, will you let me use your testimony for this book? I will change your name so that you won't have any legal problems. I will be careful so that God receives all the honor and glory."

"I will let you use my story," Fausto answered. "I have changed, and though I am ashamed of my past, I am glad to say that now I am a Christian and serve the Lord. If God can use my testimony, I will be very happy. Maybe it can help some soul be saved, too."

As the two men talked, Vicente came and joined them.

Fausto spent an hour and a half talking about all the things that had happened to him on those two memorable nights, and all that had happened to him since. As they talked and shared, bonds of love were knitting the two men together— the robber and the one robbed—two men whom God loved. The one robbed had returned good for evil, and that sacrifice helped the robber find his Master. God in heaven was smiling at a miracle so great and so sweet!

Fausto watched Pablo weep tears of joy as he told him about Rosa's Bible and the revival in the La Perrera. "How beautiful!" Pablo whispered. "All the suffering was worth it a hundred times over if souls were saved with that Bible. I can't wait to tell Tim and Rosa!"

The interview was over. Fausto had nothing more to say. The story was out. The message was clear. Yet, although Fausto didn't know it, there were still a few things Pablo wanted to say.

"May I ask my wife and daughter to come and share this sacred moment?" Pablo choked, standing to his feet.

"Sure," Fausto answered.

"Do you mind if my daughter takes several photos so we can remember this day?"

"That would be fine," Fausto agreed.

Pablo left the *rancho* to ask his family to come. The tiny recorder kept on recording. Fausto and his brother had totally forgotten that the conversation was being recorded. Pablo had forgotten, too.

Fausto whispered to his brother, "You would never see a Nicaraguan forgiving somebody who stole from them."

"That's right," Vicente agreed. "You can tell the man is sincere."

"That's right. His tears prove it. This really means a lot to him."

When Pablo came back, his wife and daughter following him, Fausto blushed again. He shook the two ladies' hands and said quietly, "I ask you for forgiveness in Jesus' name for what I did to you."

Eunice smiled back at him and said, "We forgave you way back there."

Cynthia nodded in agreement. Then she stood to one side to snap several photos as the two men again faced each other.

Fausto could see that Pablo was struggling with deep emotion. Fausto stood before him, not knowing what to expect.

"Fausto," Pablo said, leaning on the little table, "I have been waiting for this day for thirteen years. I have prayed for this moment. I have asked God again and again for an opportunity to meet one of my robbers and tell him that I forgive him."

"I—I also ask you to forgive me for what I did, in Jesus' name," Fausto choked.

"I have wanted to do two things," Pablo continued, tears streaming down his cheeks. "I wanted to tell you that I forgave you thirteen years ago. And I've always wanted to give you a hug," Pablo finished, smiling through his tears.

Pablo stepped forward eagerly, and Fausto stepped up to meet him. Both men were weeping as they embraced, and the love of God washed over them and knit their hearts together even more closely.

The special hug that had been waiting for thirteen years.

"See," Pablo continued after the special hug, "that's what makes me so happy. Most of the stories I have collected for this book are so sad. Those poor robbers, like your buddy, Paco Artola, rejected God's love. That rejection has a price, since it is such a costly love. It was not easy for God to send His Son to this sin-cursed earth. It was not easy for us to love the robbers who came and stole from us again and again. But God gave us grace to love them, to feed them, and to return good for evil. And God in heaven was watching.

"The robbers who repeatedly rejected His love paid an awful price. The price was a horrible death here on earth and eternity in hell. That's why the title of the book will be *The Price of Rejection*.

"You stole from us, too, Fausto. You sinned against God many times. And, for a time, you rejected God's love that He showered upon you through us and through others. But, because you repented and renounced your wicked ways, God has had mercy upon you. So, who paid the price that you were supposed to pay?"

Fausto nodded knowingly. "Jesus paid the price!"

"That is why your testimony is such a thrill for me," Pablo said reverently. "That is why this encounter is so precious. Jesus paid your price in full. Isn't that wonderful?"

Fausto nodded.

"And that's why we love and adore Him!"

The special encounter that proved that God's love is stronger than hatred and bitterness.

SPANISH WORD PRONUNCIATION GUIDE

Adiós lapita	ah DEEOHS lah PEE tah
Alfredo	ahl FREH doh
Amigo	ah MEE goh
Ana	AH nah
Armando Ortíz	ahr MAHN doh ohr TEES
Berlines	behr LEE nehs
Beto	BEH toh
Billetón	bee yeh TOHN
Boca abajo todos	BOH kah ah BAH hoh TOH dohs
Bocay	boh KAH ee
Buenas noches	BOOEH nahs NOH chehs
Cacao	kah KAH oh
Cadejos	kah DEH hohs
Campesino	kahm peh SEE noh
Cañita	kah NYEE tah
Cara de malo	KAH rah deh MAH loh
Carlos Picudo	KAHR lohs pee KOO doh
Carlos Pinto	KAHR lohs PEEN toh
Casca	KAHS kah
Charro	CHAH rroh
Chele	CHEH leh

Chepe Rodriguez	CHEH peh roh DREE gehs
Chepón Palacios	cheh POHN pah LAH seeohs
Claudia Chamorro	KLAH oo deeah chah MOH rroh
Córdoba	KOHR doh bah
Costa Rica	KOHS tah REE kah
Culebra	koo LEH brah
Culto	KOOL toh
Dipina	dee PEE nah
Don Lolo Lanza	dohn LOH loh LAHN sah
Don Pablo, ábranos	dohn PAH bloh AH breh nohs
Don Pancho	dohn PAHN choh
Don Pancho, acércate	dohn PAHN choh, ah SEHR kah teh
Vamos a salir con lo tuyo primero	VAH mohs ah sah LEER
	kohn loh TOO yoh pree
	MEH roh
Don Tacho	dohn TAH choh
Doña Amparo	DOH nyah ahm PAH roh
Dudú	doo DOO
Efraín	eh frah EEN
El Caño de los Martínez	ehl KAH nyoh deh lohs mahr TEE nehs
El Cuá	ehl koo AH
El Plátano	ehl PLAH tah noh
Encuentro	ehn KOOEHN troh
Esquina Caliente	ehs KEE nah kah lee EHN teh
Ezequiel	eh seh kee EHL
Fausto Sánchez	FAH oo stoh SAHN chehs
Feliz noche	feh LEES NOH cheh
Gracias	GRAH seeahs
Gringo	GREEN goh
Guaba	GOOAH bah
Guabo	GOOAH boh
Guacamaya	gooah kah MAH yah
Guardiola	gooahr DEEOH lah

Guaro . . . . GOOAH roh

Guayaba . . . . gooah YAH bah

Honduras . . . . ohn DOO rahs

Jaime Chavarría . . . . HAH ee meh chah va RREE ah

Jorge . . . . HOHR heh

Juan . . . . hooahn

Juanito . . . . hooah NEE toh

Julio . . . . HOO leeoh

Koinonía . . . . koee noh NEE ah

Kusulí . . . . koo soo LEE

La Antorcha de la Verdad . . . . lah ahn TOHR chah

. . . . deh lah vehr DAHD

La Perrera . . . . lah peh RREH rah

La poza de los compas . . . . . . lah POH sah deh lohs KOHM pahs

La Puerta Negra . . . . lah POOEHR tah NEH grah

Lapa . . . . LAH pah

Laurel . . . . lah oo REHL

Malo . . . . MAH loh

Manuel . . . . mah NOOEHL

Marcos . . . . MAHR kohs

Mariachi . . . . mah REEAH chee

Mi amigo . . . . mee ah MEE goh

Nicaragua . . . . nee kah RAH gooah

Oye, Culebra . . . . OH yeh coo LEH brah

Pablo . . . . PAH bloh

Paco Artola . . . . PAH koh ahr TOH lah

Paiwas . . . . PAH ee wahs

Pantaleón . . . . pahn tah leh OHN

Papayo . . . . pah PAH yoh

Patricio . . . . pah TREE see oh

Pedro . . . . PEH droh

Pedro Hondureño . . . . PEH droh ohn doo REH nyoh

Puerto Cabezas . . . . POOEHR toh kah BEH sahs

Que Dios les bendiga .... keh deeohs lehs behn DEE gah
Rancho .... RAHN choh
Recontras .... reh KOHN trahs
Ricardo .... ree KAHR doh
Rigo .... REE goh
Río Blanco .... REE oh BLAHN koh
Roberto .... roh BEHR toh
Rodolfo Amador .... roh DOHL foh
Ródrigo .... ROH dree goh
Ronald Artola .... ROH nahld ahr TOH lah
Rosa .... ROH sah
Sandra .... SAHN drah
Santos .... SAHN tohs
Sinvergüenza .... seen vehr GOOEHN sahs
Sirvientes .... seer vee EHN tehs
Sofana .... soh FAH nah
Tilo .... TEE loh
Tirso .... TEER soh
Tranquilo .... trahn KEE loh
Unida .... oo NEE dah
Vámonos .... VAH moh nohs
Vamos .... VAH mohs
Vicente .... vee SEHN teh
Vilma Molinares .... VEEL mah
Waslala .... wahs LAH lah
Wilfredo Sánchez .... weel FREH doh SAHN chehs
Ya llegó, ya llegó, ¡el Espíritu Santo ya llegó! .... yah yeh GOH,
.... yah yeh GOH,
.... ¡ehl ehs PEE ree too
.... SAHN toh yah yeh GOH!
Zapoyal .... sah poh YAHL

ANGELS OVER WASLALA

Tim and Rosa were headed for bed when they heard feet shuffling outside. Tim opened the door and shined his flashlight on two men, one carrying an automatic rifle.

"Money. We want $1500."

"I don't have dollars," Tim said. "I don't carry much money."

"We don't believe you. Go get your dollars." After thirteen armed robberies, four burglaries, and three anonymous letters demanding money, most missionaries would have packed up and gone home, but not the group in Waslala, Nicaragua. A true story of God's call, leading, and protection.

Yoder -- Cohen -- 250 pages -- Paperback -- $10.99

Item #ANG77900

Book Two in the Waslala Robber Series
ANGELS IN THE NIGHT

The exciting sequel to the captivating book, Angels Over Waslala! Be inspired as you read more of God's faithful protection for the Pablo Yoder family serving in Nicaragua. Amidst poverty and violence, their perseverance has brought God's light to the darkness of Waslala, Nicaragua.

Yoder -- Wadsworth -- 359 pages -- Paperback -- $12.99
Item #ANG70719

ORDER FORM

To order, send this completed order form to:

Vision Publishers
P.O. Box 190 • Harrisonburg, VA 22803
Phone: 877.488.0901 • Fax: 540-437-1969
E-mail: orders@vision-publishers.com
www.vision-publishers.com

_____   _____
Name   Date

_____   _____
Mailing Address   Phone

_____
City   State   Zip

The Price Qty. _____ x $9.99 ea. = _____

Angels Over Waslala Qty. _____ x $10.99 ea. = _____

Angels in the Night Qty. _____ x $12.99 ea. = _____

The Long Road Home Qty. _____ x $12.99 ea. = _____

Death of a Saloon Qty. _____ x $12.99 ea. = _____

The Work of Thy Fingers Qty. _____ x $27.99 ea. = _____

My Father's World Qty. _____ x $15.99 ea. = _____

(Please call for quantity discounts - 877-488-0901)

Price _____

Virginia residents add 5% sales tax _____

Ohio residents add applicable sales tax _____

Shipping & handling - Add 10% of your total order plus $3.00

Grand Total _____

❑ Check #_____   **All Payments in US Dollars**

❑ Money Order   ❑ Visa

❑ MasterCard   ❑ Discover

Name on Card _____

Card # __|__|__|__| __|__|__|__| __|__|__|__| __|__|__|__|

3-digit code from signature panel __|__|__| Exp. Date __|__|__|__|

Thank you for your order!

For a complete listing of our books request our catalog.
Bookstore inquiries welcome

ORDER FORM

To order, send this completed order form to:

Vision Publishers
P.O. Box 190 • Harrisonburg, VA 22803
Phone: 877.488.0901 • Fax: 540-437-1969
E-mail: orders@vision-publishers.com
www.vision-publishers.com

Name	Date

Mailing Address	Phone

City	State	Zip

The Price Qty. _____ x $9.99 ea. = _____

Angels Over Waslala Qty. _____ x $10.99 ea. = _____

Angels in the Night Qty. _____ x $12.99 ea. = _____

The Long Road Home Qty. _____ x $12.99 ea. = _____

Death of a Saloon Qty. _____ x $12.99 ea. = _____

The Work of Thy Fingers Qty. _____ x $27.99 ea. = _____

My Father's World Qty. _____ x $15.99 ea. = _____

(Please call for quantity discounts - 877-488-0901)

Price _____

Virginia residents add 5% sales tax _____

Ohio residents add applicable sales tax _____

Shipping & handling - Add 10% of your total order plus $3.00

Grand Total _____

❑ Check #_____   **All Payments in US Dollars**

❑ Money Order   ❑ Visa

❑ MasterCard   ❑ Discover

Name on Card _____

Card # __|__|__|__ __|__|__|__ __|__|__|__ __|__|__|__

3-digit code from signature panel __|__|__ Exp. Date __|__|__|__

Thank you for your order!

For a complete listing of our books request our catalog.
Bookstore inquiries welcome